Worldox

FOR LAWYERS

JOHN HECKMAN

ABA LAW
PRACTICE
DIVISION
The Business of Practicing Law

Commitment to Quality: The Law Practice Division is committed to quality in our publications. Our authors are experienced practitioners in their fields. Prior to publication, the contents of all our books are rigorously reviewed by experts to ensure the highest quality product and presentation. Because we are committed to serving our readers' needs, we welcome your feedback on how we can improve future editions of this book.

Cover design by RIPE Creative, Inc.

Worldox® is a registered trademark of World Software Corporation.

Nothing contained in this book is to be considered as the rendering of legal advice for specific cases, and readers are responsible for obtaining such advice from their own legal counsel. This book and any forms and agreements herein are intended for educational and informational purposes only.

The products and services mentioned in this publication are under or may be under trademark or service mark protection. Product and service names and terms are used throughout only in an editorial fashion, to the benefit of the product manufacturer or service provider, with no intention of infringement. Use of a product or service name or term in this publication should not be regarded as affecting the validity of any trademark or service mark.

The Law Practice Division of the American Bar Association offers an educational program for lawyers in practice. Books and other materials are published in furtherance of that program. Authors and editors of publications may express their own legal interpretations and opinions, which are not necessarily those of either the American Bar Association or the Law Practice Division unless adopted pursuant to the bylaws of the Association. The opinions expressed do not reflect in any way a position of the Division or the American Bar Association.

Printed in the United States of America

17 16 15 14 13   5 4 3 2 1

Library of Congress Cataloging-in-Publication Data

Heckman, John.
  Worldox in one hour for lawyers / by John Heckman.
    pages cm
  ISBN 978-1-62722-247-1
  1. Legal documents--Management--United States--Automation. 2. Law offices--Records and correspondence--United States--Automation. 3. Law offices--United States--Automation. 4. Worldox. I. Title.
  KF320.R42H43 2013
  651.50285'53--dc23
             2013041528

Discounts are available for books ordered in bulk. Special consideration is given to state bars, CLE programs, and other bar-related organizations. Inquire at Book Publishing, American Bar Association, 321 N. Clark Street, Chicago, Illinois 60654.

www.ShopABA.org

To Sarah
daughter, lawyer, friend

Contents

About the Author

John Heckman has worked in the legal industry for over 30 years and with Worldox for 20 years. He formed Heckman Consulting in 1997. For a number of years he was also a certified consultant for TimeMatters, Amicus Attorney and PCLaw, but more recently has focused mainly on Worldox. He is a member of the Worldox "Inner Circle," composed of what Worldox considers to be its senior consultants.

His blog *Does It Compute?* is a widely read source for information about Worldox and other products, and is mentioned on the official Worldox website. His Cheat Sheets and other resources concerning document management issues are freely available on his web site, www.heckmanco.com.

John's articles have widely published by Technolawyer and reprinted in including Law Office Computing, the ABA's Law Practice Today, Bar Association journals in Indiana, Michigan, Ohio, Texas, Virginia, Wisconsin, and Wyoming, as well as in Legal Times (Washington D.C.), the Legal Intelligencer, The Lawyer's PC , and Peer to Peer (Quarterly Newsletter of LawNet).

In another life, John earned his PhD in Comparative Literature from Cornell University and taught French and Comparative Literature at Brandeis and Boston University.

Acknowledgments

I would like to thank my fellow Worldox consultants for pushing me to undertake this book. Over the years, many clients have pushed me to explore the nooks and crannies of Worldox: I owe a lot of details to them. Thanks as well to the ABA LP Publications Board and staff (Denise Constantine, Jennifer Ellis, Laura Bolesta) for all their efforts in turning my draft into this finished book.

Special thanks to Carolyn Pravlik of Terris, Pravlik & Millian for her detailed comments and suggestions as well as for her ongoing efforts to "find a better way" which have helped improve my installations of Worldox. Also to Bill Baker of Baker + Cadence | Solutions for all his suggestions.

What Worldox Will Do for Your Firm

Human beings have always organized documents—from the great library at Alexandria to the 17th century undertaking by Gottfried Leibniz to organize all the knowledge in the world using a coded language that we would recognize today as a computer program. Such grand schemes resurface now in the form of "universal search," but on a practical level, how do you organize your documents?

In this digital age, the volume of information is an avalanche that many computer users spend hours vainly attempting to escape. Multiply this by the number of lawyers in a law firm, and the mountain of documents is enormous. It is not unusual for a twenty-five-user law firm to have a half-million documents. Entropy reigns.

If you think of your entire document store as an enormous book and you want to find something, there are three ways to proceed:

1. You can read the whole book. Obviously, this is very slow.

2. You can look through the table of contents. This is like scrolling up and down, in and out, of a directory structure, which is the standard method many firms use. Better, but still slow and somewhat hit-and-miss.

3. You can look up what you want in a hyperlinked index. This is what Worldox provides. It is much faster and more efficient than older methods. You don't really need to know anything about the directory structure. LexisNexis, Westlaw, and Google don't use directory structures (or at least they are not exposed to end users), but they get the job done. A computer is not a filing cabinet. You need a new paradigm. Think of Worldox as a structured Google for your documents.

What Do Firms Actually Do Right Now?

In the pre–document management system world, people were accustomed to using a table of contents (the directory structure) in that giant book containing documents. Or, to use a legal format, looking through Chapter 1, 1.1, 1.1.1, 1.1.1.1, and so on.

Many firms that have not adopted a document management system (DMS) attempt to mimic the client-centric organization that a DMS would impose. A drive letter pointing to the server is set to \\server\clientdocs, and users are instructed to store documents under some variant of "client\matter\doctype\yyyy-mm-dd-name.doc." In some cases, the IT department is even responsible for creating a default "empty" structure when a new matter is opened. To retrieve a document, users scroll through the directory tree. The amount of time spent in opening subdirectories, scrolling up and down, and poking around to try to determine where something has been filed makes this is grossly inefficient.

Virtually all larger firms have a DMS, due to their enormous volume of documents. A single person *might* be able to manage his or her own documents, but there is no way millions of documents generated by dozens or hundreds of individuals can be managed manually. Large firms have no choice but to use a DMS.

Smaller firms have been able to successfully compete by using advances in legal technology to be quicker on their feet. Why should this not extend to document management as well? Some of my best clients have been lawyers who came from larger firms and started or joined smaller firms where they insisted on having the advantages of the document management system they had enjoyed at the larger firms.

The Fatal Flaw in Manual Systems

Any manual system for managing documents has fundamental weaknesses and limitations. First, it is difficult to impossible to guarantee that *all* your electronic data—such as faxes, e-mail, and scans—are stored properly. Second, such repositories are searchable only in very limited ways. For example, you can't use Boolean operators to search for all the pleadings done from six months to a year ago that contain certain language.

But aside from these systems' weaknesses and limitations, the fatal flaw in all of them is reliance on people to follow the prime directives faithfully. In addition to staff or lawyers who "can't be bothered" or are "too busy" to put things in the right place, there is human error and procedures for scans or e-mails that are incompletely defined or not defined at all. Worldox helps prevent these failures, and the search function compensates for them if they do occur.

The losses inherent in this kind of setup are considerable: the time it takes to find something; misplaced files; not having that old contract that had just the language needed for a new one; retyping missing documents. The turning point in favor of a document management system at one firm that implemented Worldox came when, for the nth time, the office manager had to spend hours searching for a "lost" directory that had been dragged and dropped who knows where.

A common work-around is to have computer shortcuts to some of your most frequently used forms and documents. When I go into a firm and see someone's computer with a dozen or more shortcuts to specific forms or documents on the desktop, I know the person is making a valiant effort to fight chaos. But this should not be an individual responsibility.

What Worldox Will Do for Your Firm

Worldox is the traffic cop on your information highway. It organizes, stores, and retrieves all your electronic data. All documents and the "profiles" describing them are full-text indexed with advanced searching capabilities. Thus document management is a standardizing and centralizing force that maximizes the efficiency of your system. Worldox also enhances your firm's ability to meet regulatory compliance and e-discovery requirements, which may become increasingly important.

Most significant, Worldox has its own enforcement mechanism: staff and lawyers have no choice but to work with the DMS, whether they are using word processing, spreadsheets, presentations, PDF files, scans, or e-mails. Firms sometimes want to implement Worldox for occasional use. But Worldox is an all-or-nothing proposition. It is a little bit like a pregnant woman: she cannot choose to be pregnant only on Mondays and Thursdays.

A number of practice management programs with document management features and other document management programs (such as SharePoint, docSTAR, or NetDocuments) are "store and forward"—users are not obliged to use them. This means that the integrity of the data store is compromised: the firm cannot guarantee that *all* its files are stored within the DMS. This can be very expensive when it comes to discovery issues or when trying to be absolutely certain that documents can be located internally.

How Worldox Will Make Your Life Easier

Client/matter-centric approach. Many individual lawyers use the Outlook inbox as their "document management system," often storing five thousand to ten thousand e-mails there. The problem is that e-mails in Outlook are organized by each individual user; there is no automated way to locate all the e-mails across the firm relevant to a particular matter. Document management systems like Worldox, on the other hand, tend to be client- or matter-centric: everything is organized around clients and matters. Thus it is easy for the system to answer the command "Show me all the documents, scanned items, and e-mails" for client X or matter Y.

Greater speed of document retrieval. In a manual system, the user must know where an existing document has been stored and what its name is. While most users are fairly efficient at finding their own documents, searching for one created by someone else can take a significant amount of time, which is bound to be greater than the two or three seconds (or less) it takes Worldox to find something. To repeat: think of Worldox as Google for your documents.

The fact that profiles and the full text of all documents are indexed means that you can define a search using Boolean operators to see at a glance all files of a particular type that satisfy certain conditions (e.g., all briefs done in 2010 that contain the term *amputation* within ten words of *reckless*). Full-text indexing also helps in conflict checking; for example, by searching on all documents that refer to a particular business or person. When you do a full-text search and then view a file in the list of search results, it is opened at the specific text you searched for.

Avoidance of human error. The time lost in a manual system due to human error is substantial. A user may have stored a document in the wrong place by accident, forgotten what a file was named, or dragged and dropped an entire directory to some new location without even being aware of it. Worldox eliminates these errors because users are not responsible for creating a file structure in Windows Explorer when saving a document; they simply fill out a profile form with the appropriate information. When all users are obliged to use the same system, all documents are organized the same way. With Worldox, you will never lose another document.

E-mail integration. As more and more communications and file exchanges take place via e-mail, integration of your e-mail system into your DMS is increasingly important. With the current rules on e-discovery, one could even argue that it might be crucial. Having all the firm's e-mails in Worldox provides a good e-discovery base and is certainly more efficient than having some e-mails in Worldox and some in Outlook. In addition, putting e-mails into Worldox overcomes many of the problems associated with personnel turnover: new lawyers on a case have easy access to all materials.

Control over document access and ethical walls. Worldox typically gives a firm much better control over document security and access than does a manual system. Confidential documents can be made available only to the people who need to see them, whether they are responsible for accounting, human resources, trusts and estates, or highly confidential client matters. In addition, Worldox can create ethical walls if needed.

What Will Worldox Cost (Save) the Firm?

A manual system is frequently justified on the grounds that it is "good enough." From a business perspective, this claim requires that the cost of a manual system's inevitable lost time and productivity is less than the cost of implementing a DMS. For example, consider a firm where the average lawyer bills $200 an hour and loses an hour each week to inefficiency (over and above the time that would be lost even using a DMS). The firm's dollar-value losses are about $10,000 (fifty hours) per lawyer per year. The cost of implementing a document management system, including installation, customization, and training, will be at most $1,000 to $1,500 per user. When analyzed this way, it becomes clear that the "good enough" argument is actually costing a firm tens of thousands of dollars per year. The failure to make this kind of return-on-investment calculation is testimony to the fact that many law firms are still not run as if they were businesses in a time when good business practices are critical to their survival.

Conclusion

All manual and semi-manual ways of organizing documents suffer from the fatal flaw that they are to some degree voluntary. If you take advantage of the powerful searching capabilities that the Worldox index offers, you can dramatically increase your productivity. The amount of time that a document management system will save even a small firm will easily amount to tens of thousands of dollars a year. So the question is not whether you can afford to implement document management but whether you can afford *not* to. One way or another, increased pressure from clients for business efficiency will either force law firms to rationalize their practices or drive them out of business. Like dinosaurs, firms that can't or won't evolve will die.

Or, as one partner told me just a few hours after he returned from Worldox training, "I did this search and everything came up just the way you claimed it would." A lawyer at another firm noted, "I looked for this document all day yesterday and still could not find it. Today with Worldox I found it in seconds."

How to Use This Book

There are three types of comments on the point-by-point instructions in this book.

NOTES	Limitations and restrictions on how Worldox operates or variations in the tools and procedures described.
TIPS	Suggestions that can make your use of Worldox more efficient or that apply to particular situations.
BEST PRACTICE	Conventions and configurations that firm members will probably regret not following, even if they initially think there are overriding considerations for doing so.

Scope and Limitations

This book is intended to enable end users to configure Worldox in ways that will make the DMS most productive. It is not intended as a full-fledged manual and does not deal with every possible function and option. Thus it does not generally deal with options that would have to be implemented by a Worldox administrator (referred to by Worldox and in this book as a Worldox Manager; several people in a firm can have Manager status), although some of these features are referred to in the Advanced Topics chapter. The good news is that the answer to the question "Can I make Worldox do . . . ?" is almost always "Yes" (with inevitable limitations). If you need a feature, ask your Worldox consultant.

This book reflects what over the past twenty years I have come to consider the best way to configure Worldox, so some of the options and screenshots may not reflect exactly how Worldox installs "out of the box."

For readers who want full-blown manuals and instructions, Worldox ships with more than twelve hundred pages of manuals and configuration and administrative guides in the Guides folder under the Worldox program folder. These include a user manual (Worldox GX3 Pro User Guide 1 v.1.1.pdf) and a list of keystroke shortcuts (Worldox GX2.GX3 QuickKeys v1.2.pdf), as well as shorter manuals for newer functions such as Categories.

The Worldox website includes over fifty short (three to five minutes) videos on specific topics at www.worldox.com/howtovideos. Registered Worldox users also have access to a knowledge base for detailed tech support issues. And, of course, Worldox provides unlimited free tech support for technical issues (as opposed to training or "How do I . . . ?" issues).

Configuring Worldox

When you save a document using Word, Windows Explorer shows you a directory structure, or tree. Worldox replaces this with a profile group form (called File Save or File Save As) with fields to be filled in. The typical fields are Client, Matter, and DocType (documents), which correspond to what you might find in Windows Explorer when you save your files to a client or matter number, or sometimes a type of document (e.g., correspondence). However, Worldox relies on an index, not a directory tree, so searches are qualitatively faster than in Windows Explorer.

The key principle in designing a Worldox system is that what you put into it (how you create the profile groups and document types) depends on what you want to get out of it. Thus you have to think backward: start from the goal and then design the system. Normally, a Client/Matter/DocType structure is sufficient for most firms, together with an Administration profile group for confidential documents and areas (HR, financial, Management Committee), a Personal profile group for users' personal documents, and a Legacy profile group to manage old documents. Generally speaking, less is more. My rule of thumb is that the optimum search turns up just about one screen's worth of results. More than that and you may need to narrow down your search. Less than that and your search may be *too* narrow. Think of Google: how many times do you go beyond the first page (or at most second page) of results?

People who are used to directory structures as a substitute for any significant search capabilities frequently want to micromanage Worldox. After a certain point, this is counterproductive and leads not to better results but to more mistakes. If you have six different document types for motions or ten different types for agreements, there will inevitably be confusion and error.

Lawyers often tell me, "I need a directory structure because I want to see all the documents for a given matter." Fair enough, but why? A too-broad search is essentially worthless on a case of any size. If "all the documents for a given matter" turns up five hundred to a thousand files (not unusual, especially if you are integrating e-mails and scanned documents), then you have to spend time whittling them down to a usable number. An indexed search will do exactly the same thing and do it much faster.

Your Worldox implementation will benefit greatly if end users have a well-thought-out default design as a basis for adding any necessary adjustments.

The goal of a thorough preparation for installation is to get the system 90 percent (or better) complete. It is impossible to get it 100 percent complete out of the gate—there will always be something you hadn't thought of or that someone didn't tell you was needed. But if the system is 90 percent complete, users will accept that it has to be tweaked and may even feel secretly pleased when they find something that has been overlooked. However, if it is only 60 percent complete, you will get a lot of blowback, because every time anybody does *anything* something has to be fixed (or so it seems). Making clear decisions and adopting standards concerning the following options should get the firm to the initial 90 percent level.

How Many Profile Groups Will the Firm Need?

Generally speaking, small or midsize firms do not need more than a few profile groups, one of which is the main document repository:

- a basic profile group for all documents based on a Client/Matter/DocType structure (Only rarely do I encounter a valid argument for more than one main profile group.)
- an Administration profile group for confidential documents: human resources, accounting, Management Committee (Frequently this group resides on a totally different file share that most people do not have access to. The exact configuration here will depend on the firm's structure and culture.)
- a Personal profile group for an individual's personal documents (These documents should be truly "personal," not drafts or something that a person just doesn't feel like putting on the network.)
- a Projects or Workspaces profile group if the firm plans to make significant use of this feature (see Lesson 9)
- a Legacy profile group to manage old documents in the process of integrating them into Worldox
- an Electronic Court Filings profile group (Litigation firms may want to add this profile, which can be used to organize internal case dockets, making them paperless and available in a single step.)

One client commented to me: "If we had to establish this all over again, I would have a more limited profile structure than we ended up with even on our second try. The problem was that we thought about profiles the same way we thought about Windows Explorer and our billing system; instead, we needed to be thinking about it in terms of searches and what would have been best for tailoring searches."

Use a certified Worldox reseller to assist with the best profile configuration for your firm. This is a key step, and leveraging the experience of a consultant will save you from making mistakes at this critical juncture.

How Should the Profile Groups Be Structured?

There are some instances where a firm might need to supplement the three-layer Client/Matter/DocType configuration for the basic profile group. Following are some additional fields that a firm might want to include:

- Court/Venue for a firm that does a lot of litigation in different jurisdictions
- Date Filed in Court (This will likely be different from the date of the document and the "last modified" date.)
- a date field, if you need to track the date of an actual document, which will usually be different from the date the document was scanned (which is what Worldox tracks)
- a matter/submatter structure (In a relatively small number of cases, this can be useful. For example, a firm that represents real estate management companies might want to have a structure that includes Management Company, Property Being Managed, and documents for Tenants. Financial services firms may have several clients under a central organization and need this type of structure. Any firm that deals with holding companies might also find this structure helpful.)

Corporate legal departments or the general counsel of a university might also have special needs. However, renaming Client/Matter/DocType to, for example, Division/Dept/File Number or College/Dept/Matter does not change the basic structure that is needed. These configurations can also track the outside counsel that is being used for a project.

If you wish to systematically (as opposed to occasionally) track the status of a document (e.g., draft, final, or executed), you can devote a field to this. Otherwise, such annotations might better be contained in the comments field.

A firm that deals with many contracts might want to have a field listing the state governing law of contracts. Similarly, a field listing expiration/renewal dates of insurance or other policies can be useful. This enables the firm to generate a report listing all contracts or polices due to expire, say, in the next three months.

Remember, what you put in depends on what you want to get out. A typical Worldox configuration frequently represents a compromise between best practices and the firm culture and demands of specific practice areas.

How Many Document Types Does the Firm Need?

Generally, thirty to fifty document types is a reasonable number. Worldox ships with a list of Doc Types, but it's fairly generic, and firms will need to remove and add types to get a list that best suits their needs. Again: less is more. Micromanaging document types will only produce confusion.

Client/Matter Lists

Where will the firm get its Client/Matter lists? Does the firm have a time-and-billing or practice management program and want to import those Client/Matter lists into Worldox? This is frequently the case, and the preparation period offers an opportunity to review how the billing system is structured and perhaps simplify what is imported into Worldox. How will the lists be maintained on an ongoing basis? In addition to the Client/ Matter lists, you will also need a list of users, including their initials and their network logins (not passwords, just logins) in an Excel or a CSV format. It is easy for authorized users to add Client/Matter information. See Advanced Topics for instructions on doing this.

Forms Bank/Brief Bank

Worldox makes it very efficient to organize your standard forms (or briefs) into a "forms bank." This would be a separate Client/Matter listing or even a profile group administered by a forms librarian. The forms can be edited only by the librarian or other designated individuals. Users copy them as a basis for creating new documents. This enables the firm not only to systematize the use of the "best" forms it has developed over time but also to provide training for new lawyers; in other words, "these are the forms we use and this is why." It is somewhat of a mystery to me why more firms don't take advantage of this capability.

Security

Do specific practice areas need to set up security groups for their own files (aside from the Administration profile group)? Are there any ethical walls or other security requirements to prevent some users from viewing certain documents? This is an administrative issue but one that is critical for the firm to consider. Individual cases can be addressed as needed, but it is desirable to set up existing instances prior to rolling out Worldox.

Implementing Passwords

There are a number of functions in Worldox for which the firm must implement passwords; in others, setting passwords is optional.

- The Worldox administration program, which governs central settings and security, should definitely have a password.
- Almost all of my clients require a password for end users to exit out of Worldox. To maintain the integrity of the document store, it is essential that users not be able to exit out of the program at will.
- It is also desirable to require a password to "opt out" of Worldox on a onetime basis (if you absolutely had to access documents in your My Documents folder, for example). Users need to opt out separately each time they want to do this.
- The firm can also require a password for opting out of saving e-mails to Worldox, but most firms do not bother with this.

Deleting Documents

The firm may want to prohibit users from manually deleting documents. This not only prevents human error but also protects against discontented employees who just want to see how much damage they can do before quitting. To delete a document, a user changes the document type to Delete, and the Indexer application can be set to delete it automatically after a set period of time (one or two weeks). Alternatively, a Manager can delete documents manually.

Another option is to restrict the ability to delete files by sending them to the Worldox Salvage Bin, where they could be retrieved by a Manager if necessary.

E-mail

What policy or recommendation does the firm want to make about e-mail? The massive advantage to moving or copying e-mails from Outlook to Worldox is that any e-mail concerning a given matter is available to everyone who needs to work on that matter. Worldox also offers a number of other advantages in discovery efficiency; particularly as a starting point when a privilege log needs to be created. In addition, storing your e-mails in Worldox provides a major benefit when personnel changes: all e-mails are immediately available to new lawyers or paralegals assigned to a case. In the abstract, the best course is to move e-mails to Worldox (it lightens the load on Exchange and makes users' inboxes faster and more efficient). However, if you have extensive remote access to e-mail via smartphones or Outlook Web Access, you may be better off copying e-mails to Worldox so that they will still be accessible on the smartphones.

The firm needs to get buy-in from the main partners/lawyers so that it does not face resistance from firm members who think e-mail integration is "too much work."

Integration

In addition to the normal Word/Excel/PDF integration, what other programs or functions do you need to integrate with Worldox? These may include document comparison tools (e.g., Workshare/DeltaView, compareDocs, Litéra); Bates stamping; Roxio for writing files to CDs; E-Transcript; printing to PDF from Outlook; alternative PDF creation programs (e.g., CutePDF, Foxit, Nitro, Nuance); saving files from the Windows Picture and Fax Viewer or other graphics programs; custom uploads to court or other registration websites (which frequently have proprietary formats); and tax preparation software. How much manipulation of PDF files do you do (markup, combination, Bates numbering)?

What browsers are you using (Firefox, Chrome, Safari)? What versions of Acrobat are you using? Are you using other Adobe products? Are there programs that only one or two people use that would still need to be integrated into Worldox? Circulate a list and compile all the specialty programs people use.

Downloading Files

A particular case of integration that may require additional configuration concerns files downloaded from the Internet, including research materials from Westlaw, LexisNexis, and similar sites. These are immediately stored and profiled in Worldox, saving considerable effort and time. A number of websites, in particular federal and state courts, have proprietary routines that tech support may have to add to your configuration.

Document Footer

Does the firm want to configure Worldox to print a document footer automatically? If so, what should it contain? Just the document ID or Client/Matter information? Footer content can be customized on a firm-wide basis. Individual users can eliminate footers on documents that are sent outside the firm, although it is becoming increasingly standard to just leave them there.

Remote/Mobile Access

How does the firm currently deal with remote access? If lawyers simply log in to their own computers or use Citrix, there is no issue. But the firm will need Worldox/Web Mobile for browser-based, iPad, or Mac client access.

Worldox does not have a web version specifically optimized for smartphone access. Worldox/Web Mobile is an additional cost.

Mac Client

Worldox released a Mac client in the late summer of 2013. It connects to the Microsoft-based network via Worldox/Web Mobile but is not browser based. It is a full-fledged client that runs on Mac OS X 10.8 or higher. Currently it is designed for use with an existing Worldox GX3 installation, where the back end is still a Microsoft Windows server. A pure Mac shop with no Windows back end could use Worldox GX3 Cloud deployed under the SaaS model that requires no extra hardware on-site.

Initially, the Mac client integrates fully with Microsoft Office 11 and Acrobat for the Mac. It supports Search, Open, Save, and Close, and it is fully integrated with Worldox. If you are using Outlook or Mac Mail for e-mail, you can drag messages to the WorkZone (the little blue cube at the top of your screen) to save them to Worldox. Some extended features (Projects, Relations, Version Control) are still under development. The basic Mac screen is shown in Figure 1.1 below:

Figure 1.1 Worldox Mac Client Screen

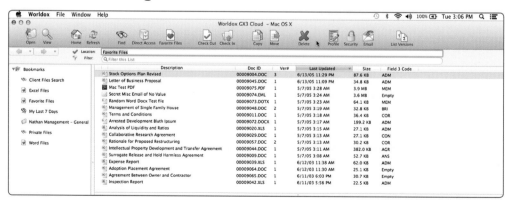

Who Will Have Manager Status?

The firm needs to decide who will have Worldox Manager status. Frequently, this is an office administrator or a tech-oriented lawyer. The Manager will be responsible (after appropriate consultations) for firm-wide defaults and settings and all the operations that require managerial rights. There should be more than one Manager, but keep the number small.

You Do Have a Consultant, Don't You?

Worldox is not a program that can be set up in an efficient manner on a do-it-yourself basis. If you don't find an experienced consultant, the firm will pay the price. Ross Kodner liked to quote the oil-well firefighter Red Adair: "If you think it's expensive to hire a professional to do the job, wait until you hire an amateur."

The initial cost of Worldox software does not include any services a consultant might offer. The good news is that once Worldox is set up and users are trained, it is rock solid. I have many clients who only contact me maybe once or twice a year for something.

Hardware Requirements and Cost

Unlike most other document management systems or practice management systems, Worldox is not SQL-based and is not very hardware intensive. A small firm will need a midrange PC to serve as the Indexer, which can also be run from your server as a virtual machine if there is sufficient space and memory. Assuming your server is relatively recent and has appropriate memory and disk space, you will likely not need a new or additional server.

There are some specific server settings and network rights issues that you will have to work with your IT people to set properly. Worldox support for the 64-bit version of Microsoft Office (and other 64-bit applications) should be available by the end of 2013.

Worldox is unique in that if you buy a maintenance contract (20 percent of the onetime purchase price) and renew it yearly, you are never charged a base cost for upgrades or a new version. Of the major document management programs on the market, Worldox is the least expensive by a wide margin.

Saving Documents

When you save a document (***Ctrl + S*** in most Windows programs) with Worldox running, Windows Explorer does not pop up; instead, you see the Worldox File Save (or File Save As) form. This is true no matter what program you are using: Word, WordPerfect, Acrobat, Excel, PaperPort, or other specialty programs that have been integrated with Worldox. The File Save form will typically look something like Figure 2.1.

You may have more or fewer fields, depending on your configuration. Some firms may also have a Typist field. Worldox uses the information in the Profile section of this form as a basis

Figure 2.1 Main Worldox Save Screen

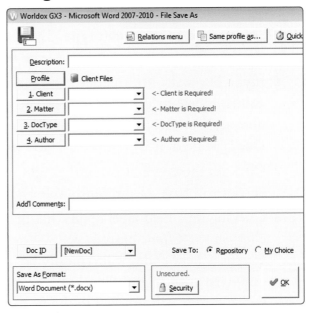

for organizing and searching for documents. The actual document names (Doc IDs) are numeric, such as 00001234.docx.

Filling In the Profile Information

Description. You have 128 characters available for a document's description. Use information that will facilitate finding the file in the future. This might be a key provision of the document, the client name, or other details. General terms, such as *letter*, *motion*, or *agreement*, or dates are essentially useless because (1) a search will turn up too many results and (2) these characterizations are dealt with by the DocType field or monitored independently by the system. If the description field does not offer sufficient space, you have essentially an unlimited amount of space (five thousand characters) available in the Comments field.

| TIP | When entering information, you can tab from one field to the next. |

Client, Matter, and Document type. There are three ways to enter information in the Client, Matter, and DocType fields.

1. If you know the information, you can simply type it in. These are autocomplete fields, so as soon as you enter enough letters to be unique, Worldox fills in the rest. Thus if you type *e* and *m* in the DocType field, it will probably show *email*.

2. Click on the down arrow at the right of the field to see a list of entries you have used recently (see Figure 2.2).

3. Clicking on a field label opens that field's list; for example, if you click on the **Client** button, you will see a list of all the clients in the system. Client codes will typically be numeric, but client names are displayed at the right. Simply start typing the name of the client and Worldox will proceed to the first unique combination of the

letters you type. You don't need to know the actual client number, although most people learn the ones they use most commonly. Normally, typing four or five characters is enough to find the client you're looking for. Click on a column header to change the sort order.

Figure 2.2 Doc Type Drop-Down List

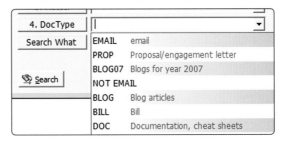

Figure 2.3 Table/Favorites Columns

TIP

There are two tabs here, as shown in Figure 2.3: **Client Table** and **Client Favorites**. The Client Favorites tab lists the last twenty clients you have worked with in the given field. If you wish to set this list as the default, right-click on that tab and select **Set as Default**. You can also have "favorite" Clients, Matters, and Document types.

Author. The Author field (and Typist if you are using that field) will probably be set to complete automatically with the ID of the user logged in to the computer or with the previous selection you made. This can be configured by your Worldox Manager. Thus you have to fill in the Author field only when you need to enter a different author from the previous document you saved.

TIP

Some firms create an Ext or External field to indicate that a document was authored by someone outside the firm. It is not, however, practical to list all possible external authors.

Security. You can set security on any document in Worldox (independent of applying a password in Word) by clicking on the **Security** button. When you select **Classify**, you see the set of options shown in Figure 2.4:

Figure 2.4 Security Classification Screen

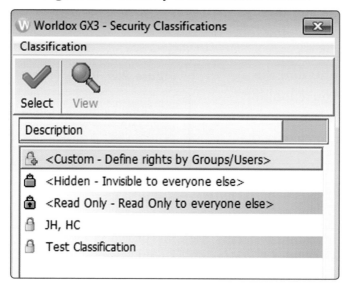

1. Hidden—invisible to everyone else
2. Read Only to everyone else
3. Any custom classifications that have previously been created; for example, by a system administrator (Manager)
4. Custom—enables you to select who may access the document and what rights they have

When you click on **Custom**, you see a dialog box similar to Figure 2.5, where you can determine who may access the file and what rights they will have regarding the document.

Figure 2.5 Adding Security to a File

The option buttons at the bottom of the box enable you to add individual users or predefined user groups. You can then use check boxes to allow specific rights.

BEST PRACTICE In many cases, particular users (partners, human resources staff, administrators) may have groups of people to whom they frequently want to assign document security. These groups should be created in a centralized manner by a Manager so that users do not have to reinvent the wheel every time they need to secure a document.

The Secret "Eighth Field"

Worldox profile groups provide a maximum of seven fields. Beyond that, you have file descriptions (128 characters) and an essentially unlimited amount of space (five thousand characters) in the Comments field.

You can also set up a table in Comments that can function as an eighth field. Litigation firms sometimes use this for entering comments such Duplicate, Privileged, Important, and so on. Other firms use Final, Executed Copy, or similar annotations. The field setup means that the comments are always going to be entered in the same way (with no typographical errors), which increases the accuracy of searches. There is a single table for all comments across all profile groups. If you need to insert multiple items from the comments field table, you must do it one at a time, and you cannot select multiple items.

Using Different Profile Groups

If Worldox has been set up properly, you will have a default profile group, but you might want to save a file or search for a file in a different profile group. Click on the *Profile* button to the left of the name of the default profile group (see Figure 2.1). A list of groups will appear. Select the one you need and proceed to save or search for the file.

You can set a new default profile group by finding the group you want to make your default in the Quick Profile section on the right side of the File Save form, right-clicking on it, and selecting *Set as Default*. That profile group will then appear by default when you save a document.

Version Control

Worldox lets you control and organize different versions of a file. Instead of having multiple files with confusing names floating around your hard drive, all the versions appear under one heading. Thus Worldox enables users to easily differentiate between draft and final versions, a functionality that has no counterpart in Windows Explorer. You can access the drafts separately and promote an older version to the newest version. Worldox allows up to 256 versions of a file—but if you need that many, you are probably in trouble.

BEST PRACTICE

Save a file as a new version when significant changes have been made—new or substantially changed provisions, not just any time you make a few minor edits. In addition, when you send a document to a client or outside counsel for review, you may wish to save that version, perhaps with a comment such as "version sent to client 8/15" so that you can easily identify it later.

A document must first be saved before you can create a version. Thereafter, when you save a new version (**Save As**), you'll see the following dialog box (Figure 2.6):

Figure 2.6 Save As Screen

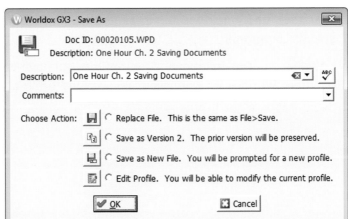

The options are fairly self-explanatory: "Save as Version *x*" gives you one higher version number than the last version. You can also add comments at this time.

When you open a document with multiple versions, you will see **Open the Selected File** (that is, the most recent version) and **Display the Version List**. You can also open the version list using *Alt + Ctrl + V*. To return to the previous screen from the version list (or other similar lists), click on the grayed-out button to the left of the current search button (in Figure 2.7, the one labeled Find: DocType=bill).

Figure 2.7 Return from Version Screen

| 🖾 Email | 🔍 Find: DocType=BILL ... 🔲 | 🗒 **Heckman Consulting - Legal\JH\0039\BILL** |

NOTE   You can access different versions of a document with document comparison software such as Workshare/DeltaView or compare-Docs, as well as with Word's native document comparison feature. This works starting either from within Worldox or from the document comparison software interface (see Advanced Topics).

Depending on how a program integrates with Worldox, version control may not be available. This is the case, for example, with a number of PDF programs that are alternatives to Acrobat. However, this functionality is being expanded; periodically check for specific programs.

Version control is not available for files that have been checked out from Worldox or when you are working off-line: you cannot make a new version when you are off-line.

Same Profile As

Lawyers frequently send documents to outside counsel or clients for review and editing. What happens when a document is returned? You may wish to save it as a version of your existing document (appropriately labeled so you can be sure which version is which). If the filename has not been changed, Worldox will recognize that fact and offer to save it as a version. In most cases, the file will, in fact, have a new name, but it can still be saved as a version. When you go to save the attachment, you will see the usual blank File Save form. At the top of the form there are options (Figure 2.8), including a **Same profile as** button:

Figure 2.8 Same Profile As Options

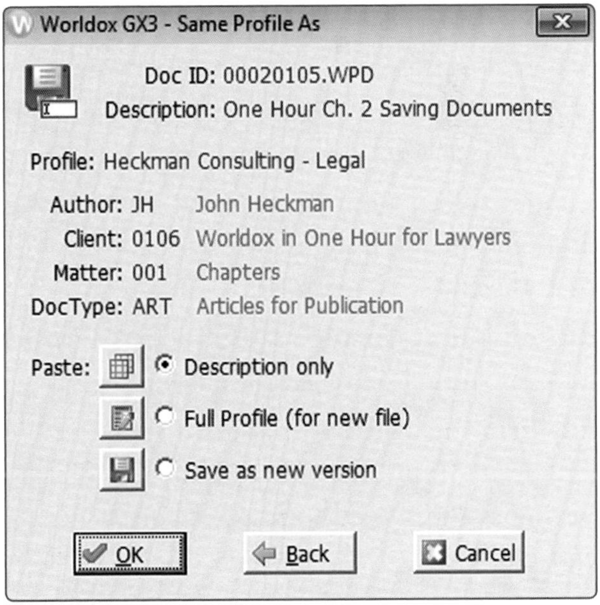

Figure 2.9 Same Profile As Screen

Click on that button. The Worldox file display appears. You can then search for and select the file that you want your document to be a new version of. Double-click on that file and you will see the dialog box at right (Figure 2.9).

Select ***Save as new version*** and then click ***OK*** to save the reviewed attachment as a new version of the document you sent.

> **NOTE**   You cannot mix document types using version control or Same profile as. For example, you cannot save a PDF file as a version of a Word document.

Quick Profiles

If you (or your firm) have created Quick Profiles, you can use them to expedite saving documents to a list of frequently used profiles (i.e., where Client, Matter, and DocType are frequently reused) by completing the Quick Profile section on the right side of the File Save form to at least partially automate filling out the profile data. Lesson 6 explains how to create Quick Profiles.

The Main Worldox Screen

When you finish saving your document and go to open another document (***Ctrl + O*** or ***File > Open***), you will see the main Worldox screen, similar to what is shown in Figure 2.10.

Your screen will be somewhat different depending on your firm's configuration, but some items will be the same. All aspects of this screen can be customized (see Lesson 8).

Button bar at the top. This lists basic Worldox operations. Most of the buttons should be self-explanatory.

File list. The columns that are displayed here depend on your firm's configuration. Typically, you will have at least Description, Doc ID, Relations, Versions, and Date Modified. Many firms also include Client, Matter, and DocType.

Bottom (Documents) bar. At the bottom of the Worldox window, this bar lists additional operations or ways to address your file list. It is examined in more detail in Lesson 3.

Navigation pane. This Outlook-style pane is displayed at the left. It can be toggled on and off with *Ctrl + T* (if you need more space for your file list display). **Bookmarks**, **Profiles**, **My Computer**, and **Workspaces** are shown here.

Favorite Matters shows the clients and matters you have recently accessed. You can open and close these listings the same way you can in Windows Explorer.

| TIP | This list can get rather large. If you right-click on an item, you can remove it. |

Figure 2.10 Main Worldox File List Screen

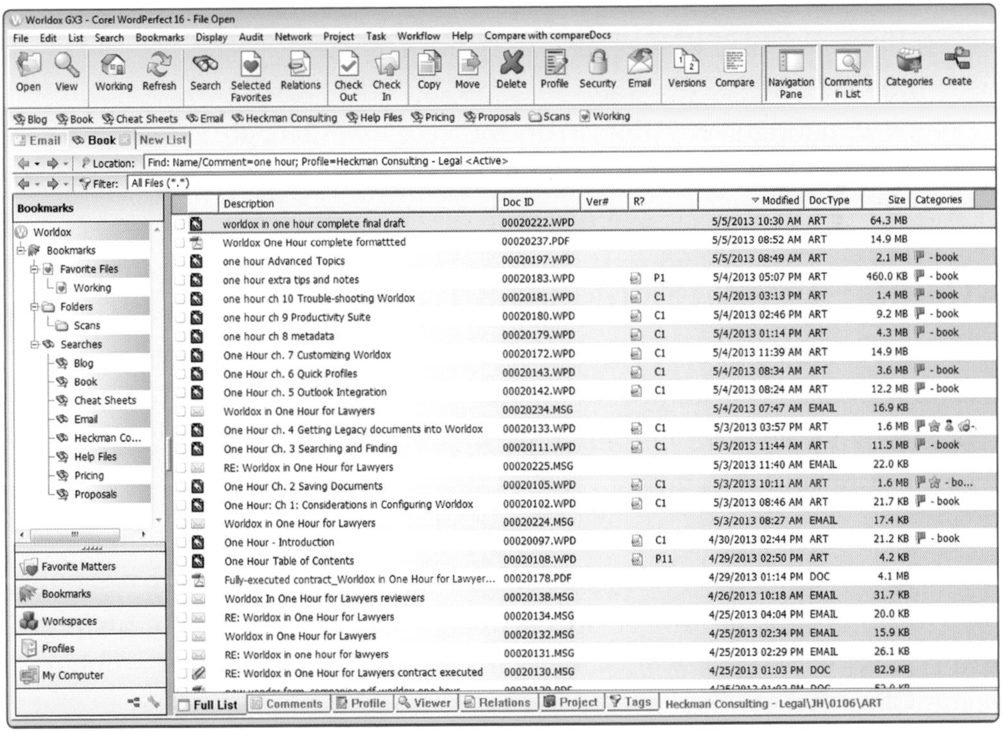

Right-Click Menu

If you right-click on any file in the
file list, you get a menu listing possible operations (See Figure 2.11).

This is standard Windows usage:
left-click to perform actions; right-
click to get options or menus. This
menu is dynamic in that selections
you have made recently appear
on the first level. However, this
level does not contain all possible
options. Click on **More** (highlighted in blue in Figure 2.11) to
see additional options. If you select
one of those, it will appear on the
first level for several days.

Figure 2.11 Right-Click Menu Options

Items with a right-pointing arrow indicate that there are sub-
choices available.

Creating a New Document Based on an Old One

The standard method of creating a new document based on an old one
has been to open the old document and save it under a new name (Save
As). Inevitably, we have all sometimes forgotten to do the Save As step and
wiped out the old document.

Worldox has a better way. Select the old document in the Worldox file
list. Right-click and select **Copy** (you may have to click on **More** first) or
hit **F8**. Fill out the profile for the new file. When you finish this, the file
will be copied, and you will be asked if you want to open the new document. Click **Yes**.

In effect, this is using Save As *before* you open the document. Following this process will drastically reduce errors when creating new files based on old ones.

Editing/Changing Profiles

At times, you will want to change the description of a document, move it, or edit its profile. If you are a keystroke person, ***Ctrl + E*** will open the **Edit Profile** dialog box. Otherwise, click on the ***Profile*** button either on the top button bar or the Profile tab at the bottom of the Worldox main screen. Change any information you want to. If the changed information represents a different directory (e.g., a different client), the file will be moved. Depending on your configuration, the file may or may not receive a new document ID.

TIP	The simplest way to change just the description is to click on it, pause, and click again. You can then edit the description in place, the same way you would change a filename in Windows Explorer. Click the green check mark at the right to save any changes you make.
BEST PRACTICE	Some firms use document types to track the status of a document—for example, Draft, Final, or Executed. If you want to do this systematically, you should consider devoting an additional field to it so you can maintain the original document type (e.g., Agreement). Otherwise, this sort of annotation can best be contained in the Comments field.
TIP	You can edit the profile of several files at the same time, as long as they belong to the same profile group. For example, you might want to add the same comment ("reviewed by JFH") to multiple files. Select the files you want to edit and click on the Edit Profile dialog box (you will be asked for confirmation). Then add the desired comment. Leave the asterisks that have been filled in automatically if you want the Client, Matter, and DocType information to remain the same.

Printing from the Worldox Screen

You can print up to nine documents at once from the Worldox list screen. Simply select the documents you want to print by clicking the check box next to each one (a green check mark will appear). Then right-click, click **Send To**, and select either **Printer** (to choose a printer) or **Printer (Default)** to print to the default printer.

If you select **File > Print List** (or **Ctrl + P**), you can print the *list* of the documents on the screen. This can be useful; for example, you could print all the exhibits for a trial or all the documents at a real estate closing.

> **TIP** Combining this feature with different sets of columns gives a powerful reporting function. If the columns do not fit your paper, Worldox offers you options to make them fit (landscape, reducing the margins and font size).

Deleting Documents

Many firms disable or restrict users' ability to delete documents. There are two main reasons for this: First, it avoids the "Oops, I didn't mean to do that" moment after a user hits the Delete key. Second, it protects the firm against any employee maliciousness (an unfortunate reality in our world).

Some firms create a document type called Delete. When users want to delete a document, they change the DocType field to Delete. The file is then deleted from the system after a specified period of time (for example, two weeks).

Another option is to restrict deletions to the Salvage Bin. In this case, when users hit the Delete key, instead of seeing the three choices shown in Figure 2.12 below, they see only a single option: **Move to Salvage Bin**. Managers can then retrieve documents if needed. Files can also be purged periodically.

Figure 2.12 Deletion Options

For moving documents from your local PC into your Worldox system, see Lesson 4. Now that you know how to save files in Worldox, you need to know how to search for and find them. That is the next lesson.

Searching for and Finding Documents

Worldox makes the process of searching for and finding your documents extremely fast and easy. Your search options will depend on how your system is configured, but the following outlines the basic procedures.

Whenever you select *File > Open* (again, *Ctrl + O* works from within any program that integrates with Worldox), you see the main Worldox screen, similar to Figure 3.1. You will probably see a list with the last twenty documents of each type you have worked on. If you have just saved a document, it will appear at the top of the list if your files are sorted in descending order by date. If you have already done a search, you will see the results of the last search you did.

Figure 3.1 Basic Worldox File List Display

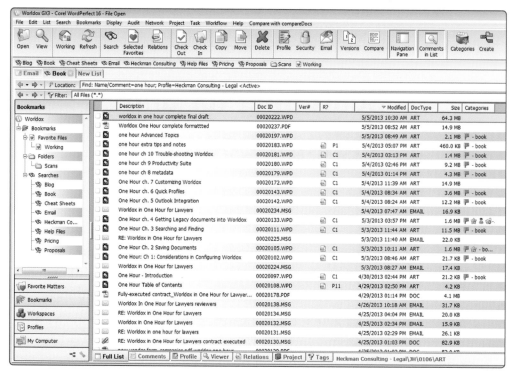

The Viewer Is Your Friend

You can further examine the search results with the viewer. Hit **F9** or click on the **View** button ![View button]. The viewer pops up and displays whatever document is selected in the Worldox file list. The viewer displays any type of file: Word, Excel, PowerPoint, Outlook, Acrobat, WordPerfect, graphics files, HTML files, and so on. If you have two monitors, the viewer will pop up full-size on the right-hand monitor. Otherwise, you can size it to best fit your monitor: drag the viewer screen to the size you wish, then select **Window** and **Save Size and Position**. The viewer will open to that size in the future.

Figure 3.2 Viewer Button Bar

As you can see in Figure 3.2, you have a significant number of options in the viewer:

- Move up and down the displayed list using **Next File** and **Previous File** (also *Ctrl + N* for the next file or *Ctrl + U* to move up, or just click on a different document).

- Copy and paste: Select text in the viewer and copy it (*Ctrl + C* or right-click and *Copy to Clipboard*). Hit *Escape* twice (or click on the red *X* button in the upper right corner) and hit *Ctrl + V* to paste the text you have copied into the document you are working on. This lets you assemble paragraphs, provisions, or boilerplate text that you want to copy from an old document into a new document without ever having to actually open the document you are copying from.

- Print the document directly from the viewer without having to open it.

NOTE Printing documents with complex formatting from the viewer may not be completely accurate, but in most cases the result should be adequate.

- Search for text within the document displayed in the viewer.

TIP If you have done a full-text search, the viewer will open with the first "hit" highlighted, and you can proceed from hit to hit (click on **Next Occurrence**). Documents that have been secured with a password are not full-text indexed and will not respond to that search.

- If you are viewing a graphic, you can size it to fit the window by clicking on **Fit to Window**.
- If you are viewing an e-mail, you can reply to it or forward it, or you can open it directly through Outlook. Replying and forwarding can be iffy, depending on your Outlook configuration. If you have problems, click **Open** to open the e-mail in Outlook and process it from there.

Manipulating the Worldox Display Screen

All columns in the display are sortable. Click on any column header and that column will sort in ascending or descending order. The blue arrow (see Figure 3.2a) indicates the order of the column that is sorted.

I usually set documents in descending order by date modified (most recent first). If you hold down the Ctrl key when clicking on a new column, it is automatically sorted in descending order.

Figure 3.2a Sort A-Z or Z-A Listed on Button

NOTE	By default, Worldox groups modified items similarly to Outlook: "Today, 4 days ago," and so on. If your documents are sorted in descending order, you may find this unnecessary and a waste of valuable space (I know I do). You can turn this off in Worldox by right-clicking on the **Modified** column and selecting **Hide Groupings**. When they are hidden, the menu will display **Show Groupings**, if you wish to toggle them back on again.

You can search within the file list. If you simply start typing anywhere (you don't have to do anything special), you will find matching characters in the list (in the description and comments, for example). Worldox will go to a description as soon as what you type matches any subset of characters in the description. The files do not need to be sorted by the Description field to do this.

You can toggle the display of comments on and off by hitting *Shift + F6* or selecting *Display > Show/Hide > Comments in List*. For other ways to make more permanent changes to the display, see Lesson 8.

You can also sort the list by a second column. Right-click on the column header and choose *Set Multi-Level Sort*. The dialog box shown in Figure 3.3 will appear.

Figure 3.3 Multi-Level Sort Options

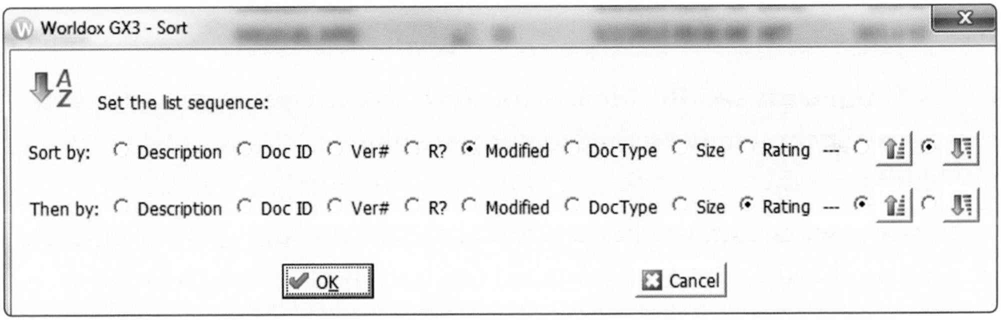

Select the fields you want to sort by and the sort order (ascending or descending). Then click *OK*.

To do a new search within only that list, go to the main screen and click on *Search* (the binoculars icon) in the top button bar and then select *Modify Last Search*. At the bottom of the search box, there is a **Search What** button. Click on it and you will see the choices shown in Figure 3.4. Select *Current List* to search the list you just sorted.

Figure 3.4 "Search What?" Options

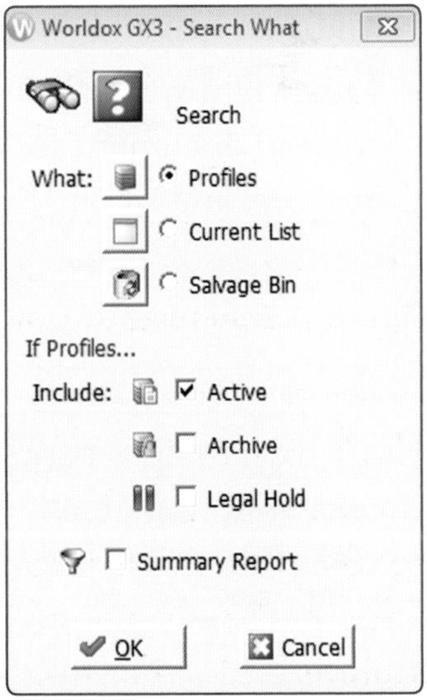

Bottom (Documents) Bar

At the bottom of the main screen, there is a bar with a number of options (Figure 3.5):

Figure 3.5 Bottom (Documents) Bar

Full List
Comments
Profile
Viewer
Relations
Project
Tags

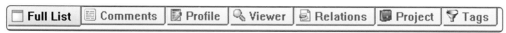

- **Full List** displays only the list of files.
- **Comments** and **Profile** let you view those elements and edit them on the fly simply by double-clicking on them.
- **Viewer** shows you the top of the current document. Since this display only shows the very top of the document—for example, the letterhead—I find **View** on the top button bar more convenient.
- **Relations** and **Project** show documents included in those functions, which facilitate building a table of contents; for example, in a closing binder for a real estate transaction or a list of exhibits for a trial. See Lesson 9 for details.
- **Tags** will display all the documents in the list according to various criteria: document format, document type, matter number, client number, and so on (Figure 3.6):

Figure 3.6 Filter List Options. Larger Size Means More Documents.

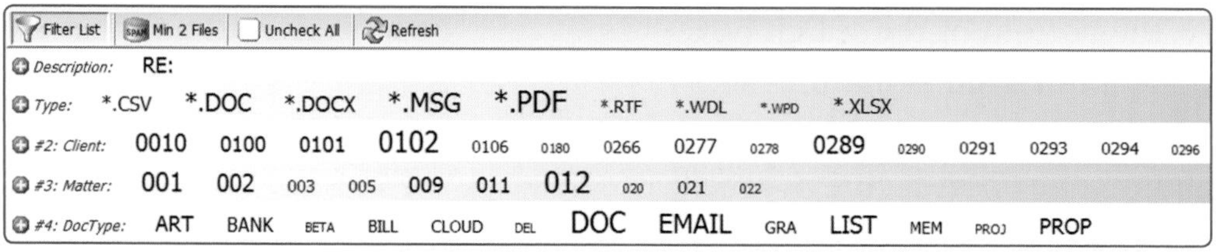

Filter List
Min 2 Files
Uncheck All
Refresh
Description: RE:
Type: *.CSV *.DOC *.DOCX *.MSG *.PDF *.RTF *.WDL *.WPD *.XLSX
#2: Client: 0010 0100 0101 0102 0106 0180 0266 0277 0278 0289 0290 0291 0293 0294 0296
#3: Matter: 001 002 003 005 009 011 012 020 021 022
#4: DocType: ART BANK BETA BILL CLOUD DEL DOC EMAIL GRA LIST MEM PROJ PROP

If you select one filter (for example, only *.PDF), you will see only documents of that type. This lets you narrow down your search to just those files you need. Whatever filters you click on, the search will find all files that fit those criteria. Click ***Uncheck All*** at the top of this window to reset. (The larger fonts indicate that there are more documents of that type.)

> **NOTE** If one of the bottom windows stays open, it may be that a Worldox Windows Style was defined with this option. To change this, see Lesson 8.

Starting a New Search

If the document you are looking for does not appear on the list when you first do a ***File > Open***, you need to find it. You can click ***Search*** (the binoculars) on the top button bar (or ***Ctrl + F***), select the profile group, and start a search. Hopefully, you or your firm will have saved bookmarks (similar to bookmarks in a browser) displayed just below the top button bar. See Lesson 8 to learn how to create bookmarks in Worldox. My saved bookmarks bar looks like Figure 3.7:

Figure 3.7 Example of Bookmarks Bar List

Blog Book Cheat Sheets Email Heckman Consulting Help Files PCLaw Bills Pricing Proposals Scans Working

Using Search is a two-step process: (1) select among various search options and then (2) perform the search you want. Using saved bookmarks is a one-step process: click on a bookmark and the search options appear or the search is performed directly. Therefore, using bookmarks for searches you do on a regular basis is much more efficient than using Search.

When you start a regular search, you see a dialog box very similar to the File Save form (see Figure 2.1). The options for entering Client, Matter and DocType are identical. As with the File Save form, you can tab from field to field. In addition, you can do a date range search.

Figure 3.8 Date Range Search

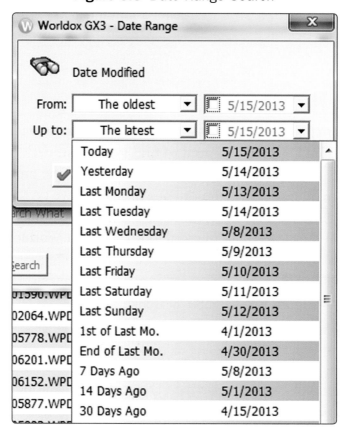

If you click on the **Date Modified** button, you get a data search dialog box (see Figure 3.8 above) that lets you specify a date range from oldest to newest. There are a number of preset options. Alternatively, you can click in the right-hand field and enter a date manually.

There are substantial additional search capabilities in the search dialog box. You can narrow down a search by entering data in fields. In the profile fields, these terms can be connected by *and* or *or*. In Figure 3.9, the connector is shown as the **AND** button. Clicking on the connector changes the criteria from *and* to *or*, or vice versa.

Figure 3.9 Basic Find Files Screen

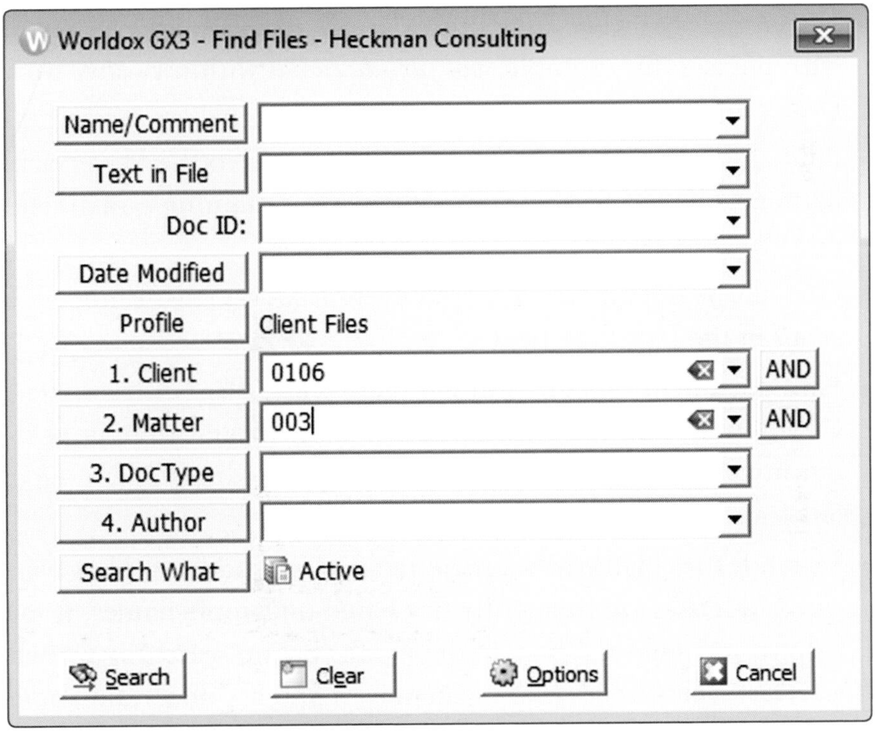

If text is entered in both the Name/Comment field and the Text in File field, this is an *and* search only. In addition, searches in the Text in File field are not case sensitive.

The Worldox search has full Boolean capabilities: AND, OR, NOT, and "*a* W/*x* words of *b*" are common Boolean search connectors. Here are some examples of ways you can use the search function:

- Find all documents with *tax** in the description (i.e., *tax, taxes, taxing, taxed*) and that contain 2004 in the file (the Text in File field).

- Find all pleadings that contain *malpractice* within ten words of *negligence* and that were done in the last six months. This also works with phrases; for example, *not jurisdictional* within twenty words of *failure to state*.

- Find all the e-mails from John Smith relating to the Haversack matter. (You will need a search template containing e-mail fields to do this. See Lesson 8.)

- Find all the documents for a matter but *not* e-mails. Enter *NOT email* in the DocType field.

- Find document types by joining them with OR. For example: *agree* OR *contract*. You can string together a significant number of these, but it will become impractical well before the limit of 256 characters for the total query.

- Search for the name of a person in an e-mail address. However, since addresses are frequently not based on simple names, it may help to surround the part of the name you are searching for with asterisks: **heckman**. More generally, if you are uncertain about spelling or want to find all word endings (e.g., *intent, intention, intended*), an asterisk will find all spellings that follow it—in this example, you would enter *inten**.

NOTE If you simply type two words in the Description or Comments field without any Boolean connector, Worldox assumes that they are within three words of each other.

TIP You can also select multiple items by clicking on the check box at the left of each one. A green check appears (Figure 3.10).

Figure 3.10 Examples of Selecting Items

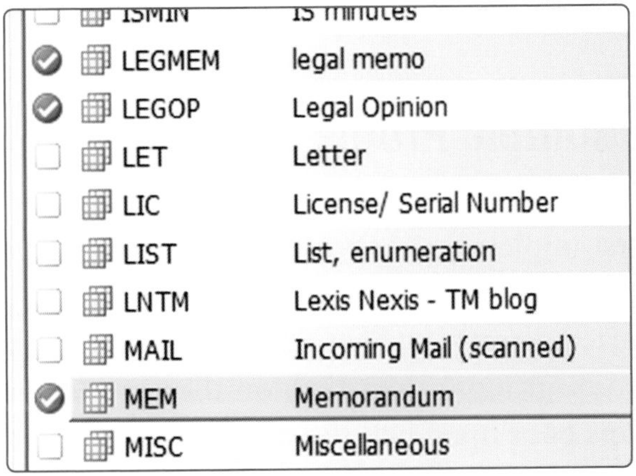

This puts all the items in one field; for example, DocType. It is an OR search: all items of every DocType will be found.

NOTE Worldox creates a full-text index of all documents that are searchable. However, it obviously cannot index PDF documents that have not been run through optical character recognition (OCR) to make them searchable. In addition, Worldox does not index any documents that have been secured with passwords; it does not try to do an end run around any other security that may have been applied. For example, income tax return files typically have passwords: Worldox will not index these.

Experiences with Google and major legal search engines such as LexisNexis or Westlaw have familiarized people with the idea that a well-constructed search is something of an art. You may have to experiment a bit to get the best results. If you use complex searches for legal research, you can use the same techniques in Worldox.

In my opinion, the ideal search turns up less than one full screen of hits. If there are more results, they are hard to manage; if there are fewer, then you may not have gotten all the relevant hits. Once the list of hits is on your screen, there are a number of ways to manipulate the results, as described above.

Searching Multiple Profile Groups

Sometimes you may want to search multiple profile groups at once—particularly after first implementing Worldox, when you need to search both your legacy documents (typically available via the Legacy profile group) and those organized directly by Worldox. To do this, start a normal search in one of the profile groups. Then click on the *Profile Group* button. A list of your groups pops up. Click the check box at the left of each profile group you want to search. Then click the large green check mark on the button bar to confirm the groups and do the search.

> **NOTE**   When you search multiple profiles, you can search only the fields that are identical across all the profile groups. If you are searching both the Legacy profile group and your main Worldox profile group, you may be limited to document names (descriptions) and full text since legacy files are not otherwise profiled.

Scanned Documents

Many firms scan documents to a specified directory on the network (or to someone's e-mail, which is much less efficient). You can set up a bookmark to the directory for your scans. See Lesson 8 on creating bookmarks.

> **BEST PRACTICE**   Use the viewer to check the results of a given scan (which typically has a meaningless name, perhaps starting with the date), and then move the scan to Worldox. The scans directory should function as a temporary "holding pen" until scans are moved to Worldox.

Locating a Document by Doc ID

If you know the document ID (for example, if the firm prints IDs as footers), you can find a file very rapidly by simply typing its ID into the Location bar shown in Figure 3.11.

Pressing F2 puts the cursor in this field. You do not need to type in any leading zeros or the document extension (e.g., *.docx).

Figure 3.11 Direct Access Input

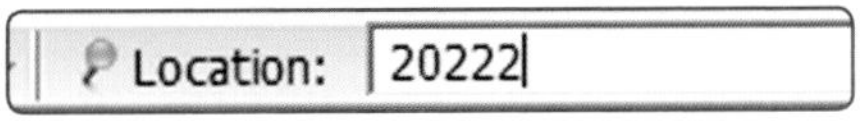

Location: 20222

Reusing Previous Searches

Similarly, you can reuse a recent search by clicking on the down arrow to the right of the Location bar (Figure 3.12). Then simply click on the search you want to reuse to select it.

Figure 3.12 Recent Searches in Direct Access "Location" Field

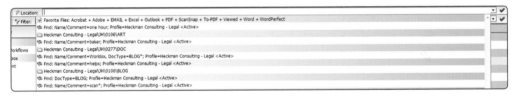

Direct Access

Worldox also has what it calls Direct Access search. While on the Worldox file list, use **Ctrl + O** to open a Direct Access search.

This search is somewhat limited in that it applies only to fields that are also directories. So if your DocType field is not a directory, you cannot use Direct Access to search for it. Similarly, Direct Access cannot search other supplemental fields you might have that are not directories.

Crawling the Directory Structure

Many lawyers are attached to their existing directory structures. These systems typically developed to compensate for the fact that searching was previously inefficient, if not impossible. Becoming accustomed to searching—like using Google—rather than crawling through many levels of directory structures looking for a document is vastly more productive. Lawyers need to be flexible in the practice of law because laws change all the time; some of this flexibility should be applied to implementing new software, such as Worldox. With qualitatively better options available to them, it has always been a mystery to me why lawyers would insist on working in the most inefficient way possible.

However, Worldox does let you crawl the directory structures of both the new Worldox files and your old Legacy documents. For details on how to do this, see the next lesson.

Getting Your Legacy Documents into Worldox

If you are upgrading from a previous document management program, you may be able to convert all your old documents and move them into Worldox. Usually, though, firms have their old files in some sort of individual or networked directory structure. They may be organized roughly by client or matter, but more frequently they are spread across all sorts of inconsistent directories, including the C: drives of users' computers.

In twenty years of working with Worldox, I have never seen a case where it was worth the time and money to import *all* a firm's legacy documents into Worldox. However, you might want to invest some time (perhaps on a weekend) to move all the files of particularly active cases.

The reason for this is simple: with the possible exception of start-up firms, a very large percentage of most firms' existing documents (70 to 80 percent or more) will never be accessed again (or only extremely rarely), so it is simply not time or cost effective to import all of them. Do you really need all those outdated drafts from an old case? If you do, you always have the full-text search option (think of it as the "Google option").

Instead of trying to import all your documents, Worldox moves the exact structure of your existing files into a "legacy" folder that is full-text indexed. The documents can then be accessed and imported into Worldox as desired. Since your legacy documents will in all likelihood not be organized in a way that Worldox can use, searches will be limited to fully indexed names and the entire text of the existing files.

The legacy searches will also be limited by inconsistent naming practices (will all documents concerning the Jones matter have "Jones" in the title?), so a full-text search may be your best option. A full-text search may also help to locate documents that were previously misfiled.

Legacy searches are one instance where crawling the directory structure may be the best way to go. To view the directory structure on your computer or in your profile groups, look in the navigation pane (Figure 4.1), on the left side of the Worldox main screen (similar to Outlook).

If it is not already open, click the ***Navigation Pane*** button (typically the second or third button from the right on the top button bar). ***Ctrl + T*** will toggle the navigation pane (formerly called a tree pane or path tree, hence Ctrl + T) on and off.

At the bottom of the navigation pane, you will see a series of options: **Favorite Matters**, **Bookmarks**, **Workspaces**, **Profiles**, **My Computer**. As you hover over the navigation pane, the options expand for easier viewing. Select ***Profiles*** and then the Legacy profile group, which will be a directory similar to the one in Figure 4.2.

Figure 4.1 Navigation Pane with Profile Group Showing

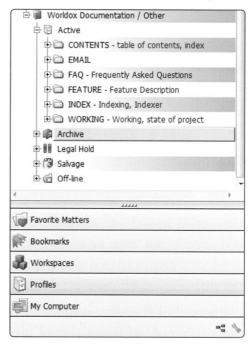

This directory works just like Windows Explorer on steroids. You can scroll up and down and open the folders and subfolders.

If you prefer to scroll through the original directory structure for your documents—they may be moved to Worldox's "legacy" directory, but the old structure will remain intact—you can select My Computer, locate the relevant drive letter and directory, and scroll around to your heart's content. Both of these options serve the same purpose.

Figure 4.2 Example of Legacy Files Directories

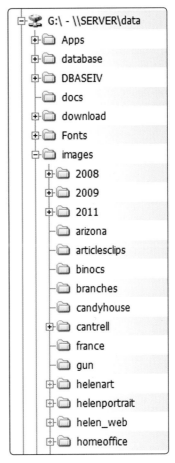

Getting Legacy Documents into Worldox

When you locate a legacy document in its original directory, you have several options.

You can view it (see "The Viewer Is Your Friend" in Lesson 3), and from within the viewer cut and paste a selection into a new document. After you select and copy the text, hit *Escape* twice to return to your original document and paste the text into it.

You can also print the file, although files with complex formatting may not print exactly right.

However, when you try to open a legacy document, Worldox prompts you to move it into the Worldox system. The reason for this is that there should not be two copies of the same file, one in the old location and one in Worldox. You *must* move the document into Worldox to work on it.

Moving Documents in Batches

You can move documents in batches as long as the destination for each of the documents has the same information (Client, Matter, DocType). Thus if you have a correspondence folder in your old structure, you can move all the documents in it to a DocType of Correspondence for a given client or matter in Worldox.

> **NOTE**   You can only move documents in one folder at a time; you cannot move documents in subfolders as well. There is a default limit of moving one hundred documents at a time (although this can be increased by the Worldox Manager).

Inevitably, however, some documents in a given folder do not really belong there, or the folder structure does not correspond exactly to your document types in Worldox. For example, you might have just a generic client or matter folder with limited subfolders. There are basically two ways to deal with this situation.

First, you can go through the folder, sort out the documents, and move the folder in smaller pieces. Obviously, this can be rather time-consuming. On the other hand, it might be worth it to weed out some of the garbage.

Second, the firm could create a document type called Imported. You could then move larger numbers of documents and sort out exactly where they should go later. This is obviously faster initially but depends on doing the appropriate cleanup and reorganization afterward.

Which option is better depends on the demands of the firm, personal preferences, and time constraints.

WorkZone

On your desktop, by default at the top center of your screen, you will see a small icon that looks like a Borg cube (to *Star Trek* fans). This is the WorkZone.

The WorkZone's function is simple: you can drag and drop any document from anywhere on your computer on top of the WorkZone, and it will be copied into Worldox. When you hover your mouse over the icon, the WorkZone changes to a file folder, and when you release the document, the WorkZone File Save As form opens up, letting you copy it. You can copy multiple files at the same time as long as they will all be profiled the same way. In that case, the original name of each document appears in the Description field.

This is a good way to copy into Worldox all the documents that have shortcuts on your desktop. If you add something consistent—for example, *zzz*—to the Description or Comments field when you do the copying, you can easily find them all as a group by searching for *zzz*.

The WorkZone can be toggled on and off by right-clicking on the Worldox icon in your system tray and selecting *Disable/Enable WorkZone*.

If you want to move documents (as opposed to copying them) to Worldox from your C: drive or any other directory, such as a user directory on the network, make sure the navigation pane is open (remember, **Ctrl + T** toggles it open or closed). Select *My Computer* and scroll through the directories to find the files you want to move. If you do not see the My Documents directory, it may have been turned off in the Worldox configuration. Check with your Worldox Manager.

Right-click on a document and select *Move*, or click on the *Move* button on the top button bar.

TIP

You should not use WorkZone to drag and drop e-mails to Worldox. Doing so changes the dates on the e-mails. It is much better to use the Outlook drop folders, which retain the date integrity. More detailed information on e-mail integration is contained in the next lesson.

Outlook E-mail Integration

Worldox integrates fully with Outlook and to lesser degrees with Group-Wise, Lotus Notes, and Gmail (via the Outlook interface).

General Considerations on Managing E-mail

The overwhelming advantage to integrating your e-mail into Worldox is that all e-mails concerning a given client or matter are available to every-one in the firm, regardless of who sent or received them (assuming the users have the necessary rights). No more yelling down the hall or unnec-essarily copying e-mails to internal people. Putting e-mail into Worldox also overcomes many of the problems associated with personnel turnover: new lawyers or paralegals on a case have easy access to all materials. For litigation firms especially, integrating e-mail into Worldox provides a good e-discovery base. So Worldox should become the primary tool for organiz-ing and searching e-mails.

Attachments are automatically sent to Worldox along with their e-mails, and the firm should set Worldox to index the attachments. If you need to edit an attachment, you can save it as a separate document. This preserves an audit trail linking e-mails with documents.

Should you copy or move e-mail to Worldox? In the abstract, it is more efficient to move e-mail to Worldox (which deletes it from Outlook). Individual e-mails will be better organized and easier to find, and moving them relieves pressure on your Outlook/Exchange system. However, there are two issues to consider:

- Many lawyers get very nervous if they cannot access their e-mail through Outlook (even if they have ten thousand unsorted e-mails and "access" is a relative term).

- More important, for lawyers accustomed to accessing their Outlook inbox via Outlook Web Access or a smartphone, when e-mails are moved to Worldox they are no longer available in Outlook or via OWA or smartphone unless the lawyers connect to their office PC remotely.

Therefore, many firms prefer, at least initially, to have users copy e-mails to Worldox and retain the originals in Outlook.

The way that e-mail integration works is subject to a number of settings at the firm level. You may want to consult your Worldox Manager, whose job is to make sure the firm has policies in place that protect its needs. In particular, consider the following:

- A Manager can set whether the default is to copy or move e-mail to Worldox.

- A Manager can prevent people from exiting the prompt to integrate e-mail into Worldox by setting a password that users would need to know to exit. Most firms don't implement this option.

- Some firms exclude internal e-mails from being saved to Worldox. However, since many internal e-mails are likely to be related to various matters, this can be problematic.

- Users have an option to exclude e-mail with personal contacts from the pop-up asking them to profile the e-mail to Worldox.

Many firms also use practice management programs that include e-mail integration. I am frequently asked, "Where should we store our e-mails: in the practice management program or in Worldox?" The answer to this question depends on the firm and involves a trade-off.

Worldox typically does a *much* better job of handling attachments to e-mails than practice management programs. In addition, litigation firms with discovery obligations would do well to include all e-mails in Worldox. This is the recommended "best practice."

On the other hand, practice management programs may have the ability to associate e-mails with individual contacts, which Worldox cannot do (although it is very easy to find all e-mails to or from a specific person).

Some firms implement both options, others have a primary program for e-mails and then selectively also store e-mails in a secondary program. However, this can get very confusing and time-consuming (naturally, you will constantly be looking for an e-mail in the "wrong" place).

Best Practice on Naming E-mails

By default in Worldox, the subject line of an e-mail becomes its description. However, after many back and forth exchanges, the subject line notoriously comes to have little or no relation to the e-mail's actual content. Therefore, when you profile an e-mail to Worldox, it is a good practice to think about changing the subject line to something useful and easy to search for. In addition, you might want to include the date the e-mail was actually sent (usually, but not always, the same as the date modified). The original subject line will be preserved in the e-mail as it is saved to Worldox.

Profiling E-mail When Sending It

By default, Worldox is set to automatically profile your e-mail when you send it. After you send the e-mail, a Worldox dialog box (Figure 5.1) pops up, asking if you wish to copy or move the e-mail to Worldox or ignore it.

Figure 5.1 Worldox E-mail Dialog Box

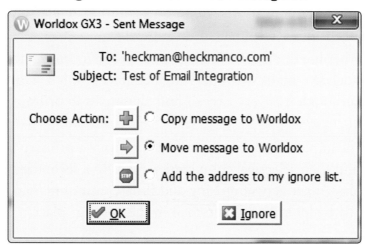

- **Copy message to Worldox** leaves a copy in Outlook.
- **Move message to Worldox** moves the message and deletes it from Outlook; it is no longer accessible via OWA or a smartphone.
- **Add the address to my ignore list** should be used for personal e-mails to recipients (family, friends, eBay) whose e-mails will never be stored in Worldox. If you add an address to this list, Worldox will not show the pop-up when you e-mail that addressee in the future.
- If the addressee is someone whose e-mails should sometimes be in Worldox but not now, click the *Ignore* button. The e-mail will not be sent to Worldox this time, but you will be prompted again the next time you send an e-mail to that address.

When you have selected the appropriate option, the standard Worldox File Save form will appear. Worldox uses "heuristic profiling," so if you have already sent an e-mail to a given person, the profile will already contain that person's information. You can also use Quick Profiles to enter information. Of course, if the e-mail concerns a matter different from the one in the last e-mail you sent that person, you will have to change some of the data.

Sending E-mails with Attachments

You can attach one or more files to an e-mail by starting either from Outlook or Worldox. Although most users are accustomed to starting from Outlook, it may be slightly easier to select and review the documents to be attached if you start from Worldox. Both options have the same results.

Starting from Outlook

When you click on **Attach File** (paper clip icon) in Outlook to send an e-mail with one or more attachments, Worldox pops up. Click on the box at the left of the file or files you want to attach (a green check mark will appear next to them). You can do this multiple times; you have full search capabilities prior to attaching files, so you can search for and attach as many as you like. Double-click on any of the selected files to attach them all. You will then see a dialog box, asking you to verify that you want to attach the files. Once you have done so, you have various options, which will be shown in a new dialog box (see Figure 5.2).

Figure 5.2 Email Attachment Options

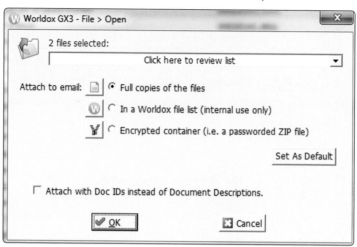

- **Full copies of the files.** If you are sending attachments outside the firm, this is the normal option.

- **In a Worldox file list.** This is for internal use only. Instead of attaching an actual file, Worldox sets a pointer so that when the recipient clicks on the attachment it opens directly from Worldox. This avoids having copies of the same file floating around the firm.

TIP If you are sending an e-mail internally but the recipient is likely to access it via a smartphone, attach a full copy of the file, because the link will not be available on the smartphone.

- **Encrypted container (zip file with a password).** This option can be convenient if you are sending a large number of files and may help avoid attachment size limitations that many firms have. If you leave the password field blank, there is no password. If you do want to set a password for the file, make sure to send the password in a separate e-mail!

NOTE If you get an error message saying that the files cannot be attached, it is probably because there is a limitation in Outlook of 255 characters for the total combined length of all attached filenames. Since the attachments have Worldox descriptions, it is easy to exceed this limit. The problem can be avoided by either selecting *Attach with Doc IDs instead of Document Descriptions* (see Figure 5.2) or starting your e-mail from within Worldox.

Starting from Worldox

To send an e-mail with an attachment starting from within Worldox, first simply select the file (or files) on the main Worldox list screen by clicking the box to the left of the description. A green check mark will appear. Then click *Email* (open envelope icon) on the top button bar or use **Ctrl + M**. Alternatively, right-click on the file and select *email*. (If the e-mail command is not on the first list, select *More* and then *email*.) Starting from Worldox when you send an e-mail with multiple attachments gets around the restriction on the number of characters in attachment filenames that exists in Outlook. In addition, if you are attaching more than one file, it may be more efficient to start from Worldox to avoid having to repeat the same search you already did.

When you start an e-mail from Worldox, your normal Outlook signature block does not automatically appear in the e-mail. You could, of course, manually attach it, but that is cumbersome. You can (mostly) duplicate your signature block for use with e-mails starting from Worldox (see Figure 5.3). To do this, click the *Email* button at the far left of the main screen, above the navigation pane. Then select *Edit > Signature from the Menu*.

To insert an existing signature, click on *Insert > Signature* and select the relevant signature. To add your e-mail signature, follow the instructions (shown in Figure 5.3), hit ***Escape*** to exit, and click ***OK*** to save the signature.

Figure 5.3 Signature Block Creation from Within Worldox

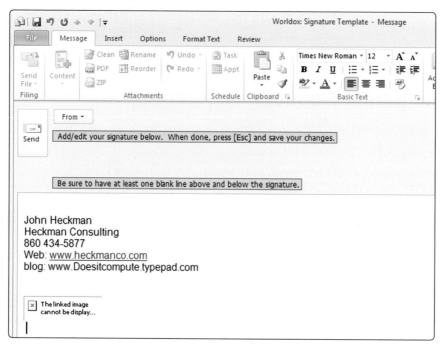

| NOTE | This works only on new e-mails, not if you reply to or forward an e-mail from Worldox. You also cannot use a graphic in the signature block. |

Viewing Outlook Information from Worldox

You have full control of your Outlook system from within Worldox by clicking on the ***Email*** button above the navigation pane on the left side of the main Worldox screen. This includes not just e-mails, but tasks, calendar, and contacts (see Figure 5.4). Modules aside from e-mail (calendar, contacts) display as lists, but if you select a contact and press *F9*, Worldox displays the Outlook contact card.

Figure 5.4 View of Outlook Inbox from Within Worldox

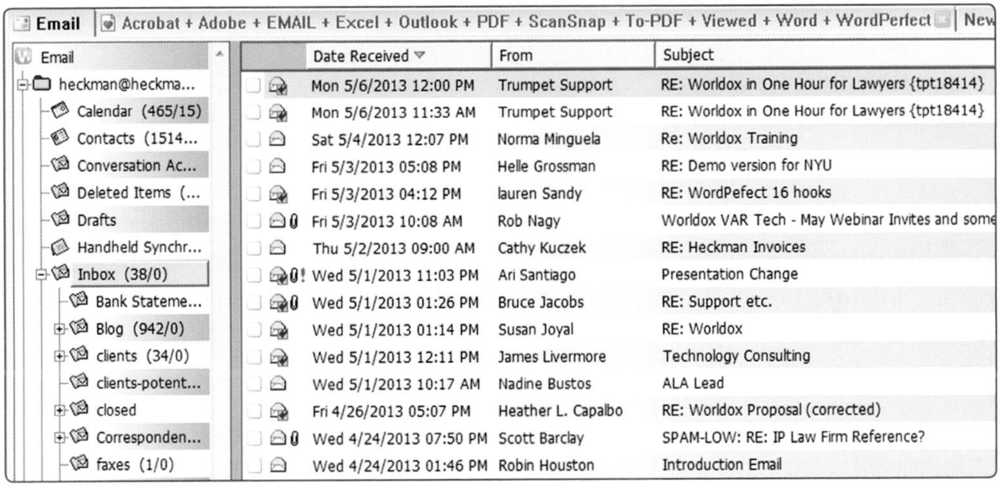

Email	Acrobat + Adobe + EMAIL + Excel + Outlook + PDF + ScanSnap + To-PDF + Viewed + Word + WordPerfect	New

Email		Date Received ▽	From	Subject
heckman@heckma...		Mon 5/6/2013 12:00 PM	Trumpet Support	RE: Worldox in One Hour for Lawyers {tpt18414}
Calendar (465/15)		Mon 5/6/2013 11:33 AM	Trumpet Support	RE: Worldox in One Hour for Lawyers {tpt18414}
Contacts (1514...		Sat 5/4/2013 12:07 PM	Norma Minguela	Re: Worldox Training
Conversation Ac...		Fri 5/3/2013 05:08 PM	Helle Grossman	RE: Demo version for NYU
Deleted Items (...		Fri 5/3/2013 04:12 PM	lauren Sandy	RE: WordPefect 16 hooks
Drafts		Fri 5/3/2013 10:08 AM	Rob Nagy	Worldox VAR Tech - May Webinar Invites and some
Handheld Synchr...		Thu 5/2/2013 09:00 AM	Cathy Kuczek	RE: Heckman Invoices
Inbox (38/0)		Wed 5/1/2013 11:03 PM	Ari Santiago	Presentation Change
Bank Stateme...		Wed 5/1/2013 01:26 PM	Bruce Jacobs	RE: Support etc.
Blog (942/0)		Wed 5/1/2013 01:14 PM	Susan Joyal	RE: Worldox
clients (34/0)		Wed 5/1/2013 12:11 PM	James Livermore	Technology Consulting
clients-potent...		Wed 5/1/2013 10:17 AM	Nadine Bustos	ALA Lead
closed		Fri 4/26/2013 05:07 PM	Heather L. Capalbo	RE: Worldox Proposal (corrected)
Corresponden...		Wed 4/24/2013 07:50 PM	Scott Barclay	SPAM-LOW: RE: IP Law Firm Reference?
faxes (1/0)		Wed 4/24/2013 01:46 PM	Robin Houston	Introduction Email

When you select one or more files, you have an option on the top button bar (shown in Figure 5.5) to copy or move the e-mails to Worldox.

The same considerations apply toward copying or moving files starting from Worldox as if you were starting from Outlook.

Figure 5.5 Copy or Move to Worldox

Copy to Worldox   Move to Worldox

Importing Inbound E-mail into Worldox

Worldox does not automatically try to profile incoming e-mail: there are too many variables to do it effectively (personal mail, junk mail).

To copy or move an e-mail to Worldox, select the e-mail and click on the **Copy to Worldox** or **Move to Worldox** icon. These will be in different places depending on your version of Outlook. In Outlook 2007 or 2010, these icons will appear when you open the Worldox menu option at the top of the screen.

You can also batch import e-mails by selecting multiple e-mails and clicking one of the icons mentioned above. There is a default limit of one hundred e-mails at a time, but this can be expanded by the Worldox Manager. There are two main ways to increase the efficiency of this process:

1. If you have subfolders in Outlook, it is likely that they are associated with matters. You can select all the e-mails in a given subfolder and import them to the "e-mail" DocType of the desired matter.

2. If you do not organize by folders, sort the e-mails in your inbox by recipient. The chances are good that most of the e-mails to the same recipient will be associated, if not with just one matter, with a limited number of matters. Select all the e-mails that will be imported for a given matter and copy or move them to Worldox. You can do this whether you start from Outlook or Worldox.

Customizing the Outlook Toolbar

By default, Worldox puts a menu item in the main menu bar of Outlook (not in the Ribbon). From here, it takes only two clicks to copy or move an e-mail to Worldox.

However, you can put the Worldox buttons directly on either the Quick Access toolbar or the Ribbon bar. The process is the same in both cases. Right-click on the *File* menu and select *Customize Quick Access Toolbar* or *Customize Ribbon Bar*. Under **Main Tabs**, you will see one that says **Worldox**. Open it and put the *Copy* and *Move* items on the Ribbon or the Quick Access toolbar.

Using Worldox to Archive E-mails

Many lawyers may have ten thousand (or even more) completely unsorted e-mails in their inboxes. One approach to resolving the problems that this causes is to mass archive old e-mails into Worldox.

For example, you could create a "client" called Archived Email with a "matter" for each user. Alternatively, many firms have personal lawyer matters under a Firm General client. Create DocTypes for 2010email, 2011email, and 2012email, for example. Then select and move all the e-mails for a given year to the respective DocType. This lets the lawyers keep more recent e-mail in Outlook while making it much more efficient to find older e-mail, since it will be searchable by the To and Subject lines as well as the year or any text in the e-mail. However, you might require a more granular approach, depending on your firm's record retention policies.

Importing Your Archived PST Files

With a little extra work, you can also get Outlook e-mails that have already been archived as PST files into Worldox. The trick is to restore access to the archive folder and then go from there. In Outlook, select *File > Open > Outlook Data File*. Open the archive.pst folder (the name may be different depending on your version and configuration of Outlook). If your network administrator has been storing archive files off-line some-where, you may have to negotiate for the ability to do this—but most network administrators will be more than happy to do anything that reduces the load on Outlook and your Exchange server.

The archive folder will appear at the bottom of the Outlook inbox and folders list. You can then open it and move those files into Worldox.

Quick Profiles for E-mail

If you send e-mails to the same person, Worldox remembers the profile information for the last e-mail you sent and automatically fills them in. If you typically send e-mails concerning multiple matters to this person, you will have to remember to review the Client and Matter information each time.

After you send an e-mail and save it to Worldox, you are prompted to create a Quick Profile. Quick Profiles contain pre-filled-in information about a document you are saving. For example, if you send a large number of e-mails to various people regarding a particular matter, you may not want to have to fill in the client and matter infor-mation every time. If you click *OK* to the prompt, a pop-up appears, asking for the name of the Quick Profile (see Figure 5.6).

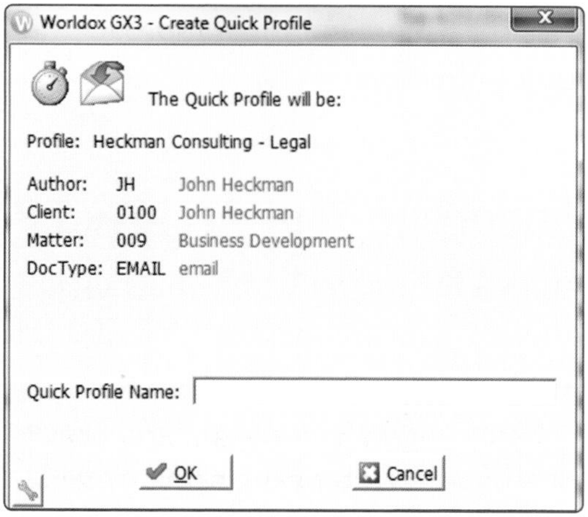

Simply type in a name. Once a Quick Profile has been created, you obviously want to avoid creating duplicates.

Figure 5.6 Quick Profile Creation Screen

When you opt to copy or move the next e-mail to that particular recipient, you can choose the information from the Quick Profile list on the right side of the File Save form if it is not already filled in.

Drag and Drop to Worldox

Click on the main Worldox folder in Outlook (toward the bottom of your Navigation Pane) and then the ***Quick Profiles*** button to add new Quick Profiles or edit existing ones.

When you create a new Quick Profile, either here or when prompted after saving an e-mail, you can make subfolders by typing backslashes (\) in the filename. When you click ***OK***, a confirmation pop-up appears (Figure 5.7). If all the information is correct, a message in green will state that the profile is valid.

Figure 5.7
Quick Profile Confirmation Screen

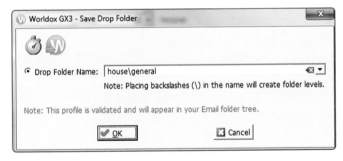

If the information is not correct, a message in red will state that the profile is not valid and will not appear in your Email folder tree.

NOTE You will see a drop-down list on this pop-up if you click on the down arrow at the right of the folder name box (see Figure 6.3), but it does not appear in the pop-up for creating a Quick Profile after sending an e-mail.

Quick Profiles created when you save an e-mail will normally show up as "drag and drop" folders that let you move or copy e-mails to Worldox. First check to see that there is a Worldox folder in Outlook. It will contain all the Quick Profiles you created when you saved e-mails (see Figure 5.8).

This lets you make a multilevel set of client/matter folders. You can then drag and drop e-mails directly into those folders without having to fill out File Save forms. By default, this operation *moves* files to Worldox; to *copy* them, hold down the **Ctrl** key when you drag them to the folder (just as in Windows).

Figure 5.8 Drag and Drop Folders

When you click on a specific folder, you may see the Worldox search results to which that folder points, depending on how Worldox is configured (see Figure 5.9).

Figure 5.9 Worldox Search Results View in Outlook

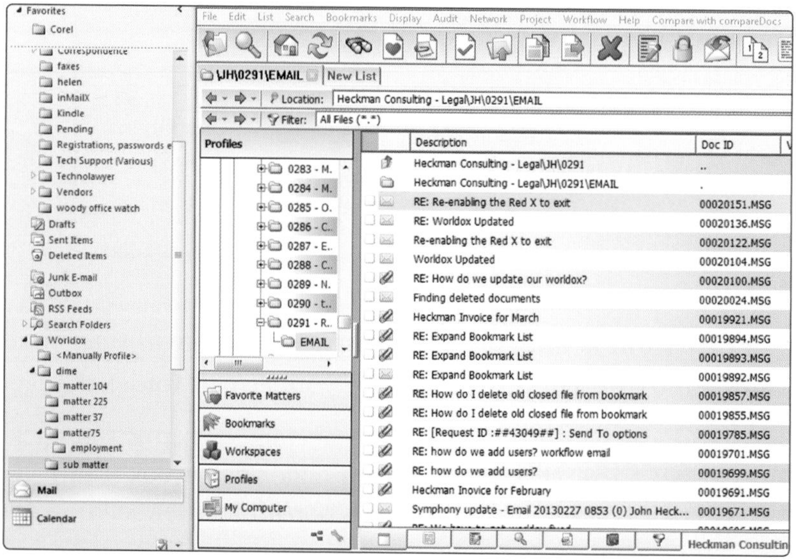

Address Rules

Address rules govern how e-mails to or from certain individuals are managed in Worldox. Assuming you have rights to do so, you can add or modify existing address rules using the commands shown in Figure 5.10.

Figure 5.10 Address Rules Screen

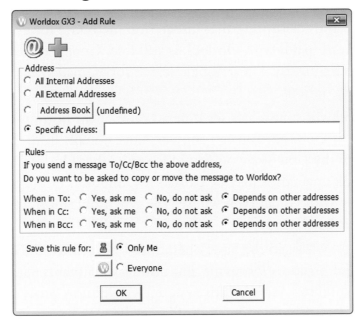

Select the **Email** button at the left of the Location bar, then **Edit > Address Rules**. You will see the list of existing rules and the standard Worldox edit options (Add, Edit, Delete; Figure 5.11). Click the large green plus sign to add a new rule. Fill in the options as desired and click **OK**.

Figure 5.11
Add Edit Delete

Note that if you do not have Manager rights, you will not have the option to save this rule for everyone.

Integrating Worldox with Gmail

Prior to 2013, Worldox could use a free link with Gmail to sync with Outlook. However, in 2013, Google dropped the free link between Gmail and Outlook, thus disrupting that integration method. However, the sync for Google Apps (paid) with Outlook is still fine. Google tends to change these settings frequently. Do a Google search for "Gmail sync Outlook" for the current options.

Your Gmail will appear as a separate account at the bottom of the navigation pane in Outlook. You can copy or move e-mails from this account to Worldox in the same way you would for any other Outlook account. Some Outlook operations may be paused if Outlook is in the process of synchronizing with Gmail (you will see the synchronization screen with green progress bars).

You have now learned the basic operations of Worldox: the best techniques and practices for saving and finding documents and how to integrate Email into your Worldox system. We will now proceed to more advanced topics, including Quick Profiles in the next lesson.

Quick Profiles

Quick Profiles are a way to automate or semi-automate filling out the File Save form when saving a document. Quick Profiles make it much easier to apply a profile to a new document when you save large numbers of files to the same matter. Whenever you save a document, you see a Quick Profiles section (shown in Figure 6.1) on the right side of the File Save form.

There are two tabs: **My Profiles**, which you have created for your own use and possibly e-mailed to others, and **Public Profiles**, which have been created for the entire firm.

Figure 6.1
File Save Quick Profile List

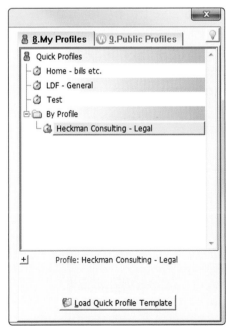

| NOTE | Quick Profiles are action-specific: you see different ones depending on whether you are saving a document or are copying, moving, or creating a Quick Profile for an e-mail. |

There are several ways to create a Quick Profile. The easiest is to first start to save a document. Fill out the information that you want to save as a Quick Profile. This may not be all the information in the profile; for example, the Quick Profile might include the Client or Matter but not the Document type. Fill in all the details that will be the same every time you save a similar document. Then click on the ***Quick Profile menu*** button (see Figure 6.2) at the top of the File Save form.

Figure 6.2 Menu Options on Profile Save Screen

You will see two options: **Add/Edit Quick Profiles** and **Save Quick Profile**. The procedures are different, depending on which option you pick.

Save as a Quick Profile. You will be asked to give the profile a name (see Figure 6.3).

Figure 6.3 Quick Profiles with Sub-Lists

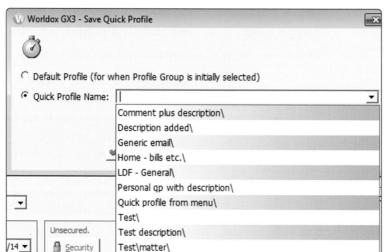

If you want to create a number of Quick Profiles for a given matter, you can create subprofiles by using a backslash (\) in the filename. For example, if you have a litigation matter and you want a Quick Profile for different document types, you can create subprofiles for \pleadings, \discovery, \correspondence, and so on. If you want to add a subprofile to an existing Quick Profile, click on the down arrow to the right of the name field to view existing Quick Profiles (see Figure 6.3). Select a file and enter the name of the subprofile. The backslash (\) has already been added.

> **NOTE** This option lets you add information to the Comments field in the Quick Profile but not to the Description field.

Add/Edit Quick Profiles. When you click on *Add/Edit Quick Profiles*, you will see a list of your Quick Profiles with menu buttons at the bottom giving you options to create a new Quick Profile, edit an existing one (put the cursor on the one you want to edit), delete one, or exit. If you click on **New**, you must first select the base profile group you want to use for the Quick Profile; then the standard File Save form pops up. Fill out the form with the information you want in your Quick Profile.

> **NOTE** With this option, you can put information in both the Description and the Comments fields.

Click *Save*. You will be asked to give the Quick Profile a name. Name it and click *OK*. The name should now appear in the list of your Quick Profiles. Click *Close* to exit.

You can create as many Quick Profiles as you want. However, as a practical matter, it becomes counterproductive after a certain point. If you have, say, fifty or more Quick Profiles, it might take you more time to find the one you want than to just fill in the profile.

E-mailing Quick Profiles

Once you have created a Quick Profile, you can e-mail it to another user so that the user does not have to re-create it from scratch. Simply right-click on the Quick Profile you want to e-mail and select ***Email to another user*** from the list shown in Figure 6.4.

Outlook will pop up and you can e-mail the file.

If you receive a Quick Profile from another user (it will appear as a WDL file attachment), double-click on it. A pop-up (Figure 6.5) will ask you to confirm that you want to import the Quick Profile to Worldox. Select the file and click ***Yes***.

Figure 6.4 Emailing Quick Profile   **Figure 6.5** Importing a Quick Profile

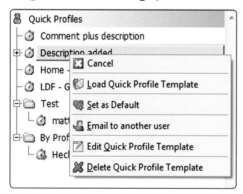
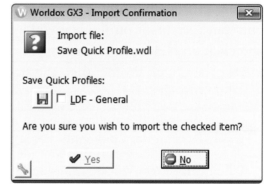

Taking Documents with You

Check Out/Check In

Most firms today are set up so that you can work remotely, from home or elsewhere. In most cases, you are essentially still working at your desk in the office. However, what if you are traveling or need to take documents out of the office for one reason or another? There are two main ways to do this, check out/in and copying the document to your hard drive or USB drive.

Checking Documents Out

You can check a document out of the system. This is just like checking a book out of a library: if the item is checked out, no one else has access to it, and in the case of a document, no other users can edit it—they can only view or copy the file. The obvious reason for this is that if you were to check out a document and edit it while someone else in the office was also editing it, then when the document is uploaded after being checked out, "the last edits win" (the other edits would be lost).

To check out a document, right-click on the file and select ***Check Out*** (or use ***Alt + F8*** or ***File > Check Out***). You will then see the dialog box shown in Figure 7.1.

Local mirror folder is a built-in function of Worldox that automatically "mirrors" or saves a copy of any file you work on to your local hard drive for seven days (by default). If you are taking a laptop out of the office, you might want to check a document out to the mirror folder. However, you may also want to check files out to send to document production or some other

Figure 7.1 File Check-Out Screen

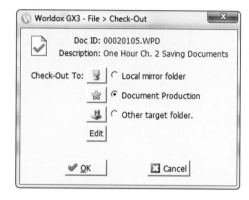

predesignated folder. If you check **Document Production**, an Edit button appears that allows you to modify where the document is going. This lets you change the name as well as the directory.

If you check **Other target folder**, a dialog box similar to Figure 7.2 pops up, and you can select where checked-out documents appear.

Figure 7.2 Edit Check-Out Target

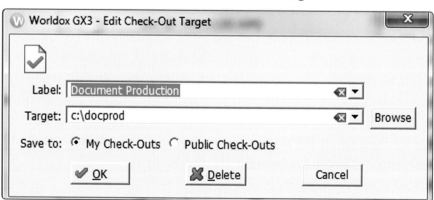

NOTE You *must* use the **Browse** button to do this; you cannot simply type in a path. You must also create the folder outside of Worldox before selecting it.

Checking Documents In

If users try to access a document that has been checked out, they see a message telling them when the document was checked out and by whom, similar to what is shown in Figure 7.3 below. Only the person who checked out the document (or a Manager) can check it back in. A green check mark at the left of the status means you are the person who checked the document out; a red check mark means someone else checked it out.

Figure 7.3 Checked-Out Indication in File List

	Worldox GX2 User Manual v. 2.0 pdf helpx	00016208.PDF
	☑ *Checked-out by Heckman, John (HECKMA) on 4/28/2013* 📋 *Check-In*	

When you reconnect to your network after being away from the office, a moment after Worldox starts up, you will see the brief pop-up notice (similar to Outlook notices) shown in Figure 7.4.

After the notice disappears, there will be an icon with a small green check mark in it in the system tray. Double-click on the icon to check your document(s) in.

When you check a document in, you have options to overwrite the network copy with your edits or to simply dismiss the checked-out document and discard any edits you

Figure 7.4 Files to Be Checked In Notice

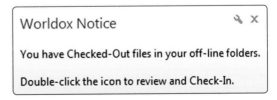

Worldox Notice ⚒ ✕

You have Checked-Out files in your off-line folders.

Double-click the icon to review and Check-In.

made. If you have not changed the checked-out document, you will see only an option to discard the local copy.

You also have the option to check the document in as a new version. If you have made significant edits while off-line, you may want to do this.

TIP If you know you have not changed the document, you can check it back in by clicking on **Check-In** in the comment under the file listing (see Figure 7.3), as long as you are the person who checked it out in the first place.

Send To

There may be times when you want to take files with you but don't need or want to check out documents. For example, lawyers frequently want to take all the documents in a matter with them to a trial or when visiting clients. They don't want to edit any of them, just have them. In that case, you can use **Send To**, which *copies* files to a specified location. There are a number of additional default options, depending on which programs are installed on your computer. For example, some PDF programs may include an option to convert a Word document to PDF. Figure 7.5 shows a **Send To** in process.

Figure 7.5 Some Send To Options

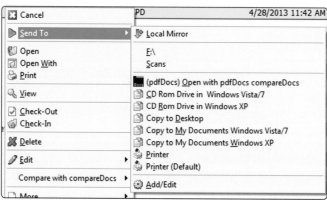

TIP — You may want to use Send To for all the files in your list. Use **Ctrl + A** to select all files. **Alt + Ctrl + A** deselects all files. If you want to select a group of files, click on the selection box for the first file you want and then **Shft + Click** on the last file you want, and all the intervening files will be selected. Alternatively, select **File > Tag or File > Untag** for options.

TIP — If you have a USB thumb drive plugged into your computer, it automatically appears as an option (the "F:\" drive in Figure 7.5).

If you are comfortable dealing with code, it is not too difficult to create additional Send To destinations or customize configurations. For example, I have several clients who have customized a folder (C:\trialdocs) to which they send all the files for a particular matter when they plan to take them to trial. You can export just the filenames or an entire Client/Matter/ DocType structure.

Right-click on any item to get the ***Send To*** menu; select ***Add/Edit*** and then ***Add***. Look at Figure 7.6 to see an example of the code to send files to a C:\trialdocs folder with Client/Matter/DocType subdirectories.

Figure 7.6 Sample Send To Code

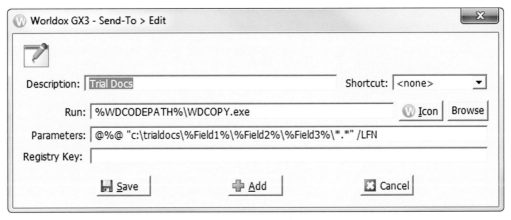

In the example, Field 1 is Client, Field 2 is Matter, and Field 3 is DocType. If you try this, make sure that the quotation marks opening and closing the path match and the percent signs around each field also match. The use of */LFN* at the end tells Worldox to export the long filenames, not just the document IDs.

> **NOTE**   Although the documents display with descriptions and comments, you do *not* have full Worldox functionality in terms of searching when you use Send To. You have to crawl up and down the directory tree of the exported documents. When you return to the office, simply delete the copies.

Putting Files on a CD or DVD

There are three ways to copy files to a CD or DVD.

1. The Send To function discussed above (see Figure 7.5) lets you copy files to a DVD (the description of this option varies, depending on your version of Windows).

2. If you use Roxio or a similar a DVD creation program, it can be integrated into Worldox. When you try to add a file, Worldox pops up.

3. You can create a specific directory: use Send To to copy files to that directory, and burn the DVD from there.

One of the main ways of making Worldox even easier to use is to customize the display to best fit how you work. That is the topic of the next lesson.

Lesson 8

Customizing the Worldox Display

When you open Worldox, you will see a screen similar to the one shown in Figure 8.1. (Your view will vary depending on your existing customization). Almost everything about this screen can be customized.

Figure 8.1 Basic Worldox File List Display

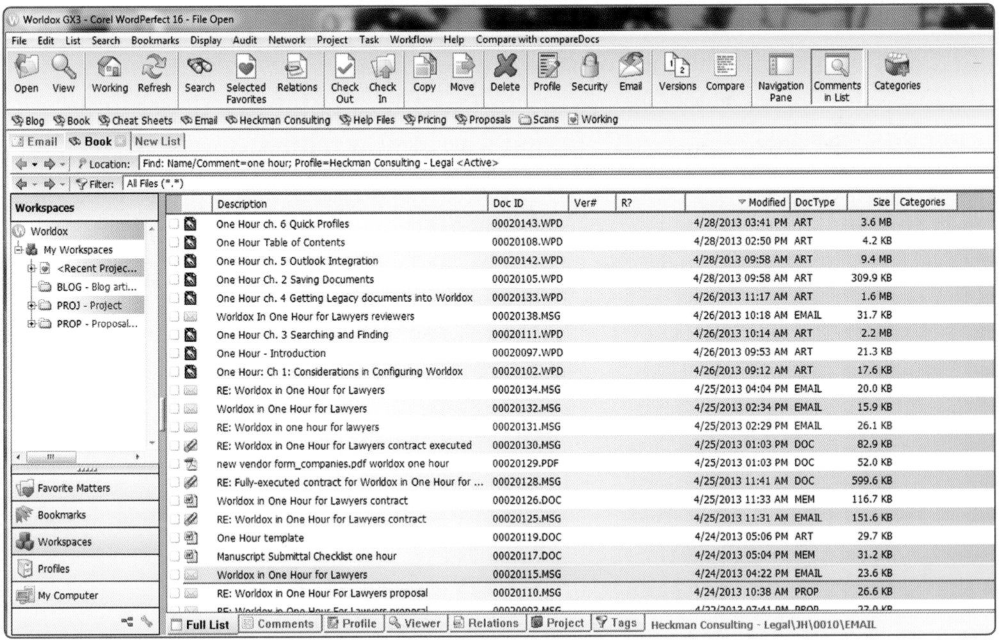

In this lesson, you'll learn about some of the most common customization options and how to use them.

BEST PRACTICE The Worldox Manager should consult with firm members before implementation to create firm-wide default settings for the features described below. Those settings will provide a baseline from which individuals can customize their displays, if they so desire.

Note that anywhere you see a wrench icon, clicking on it gives you configuration options for the area of the program with which you are working.

Column Display

Columns can be resized, and you can sort any column. Simply click on the column you wish to sort, and the column will be sorted in ascending or descending order. A blue triangle will indicate the order, pointing down for A–Z and up for Z–A. If you hold down the **Ctrl** key when you click on a new column, it will automatically be sorted in descending order. You can also change the placement and width of columns, depending on the size of your screen. To do make a column wider, simply drag the right-hand edge of the column to the width you desire. To move it to an entirely new position, just drag and drop it between other columns. (You can also create a second-level sort on the display. See Lesson 3 for more on the topic.)

TIP

Worldox is set to automatically size columns to default widths. This may not give you the best results, depending on the number of columns you have, the average size of monitors in the firm, and the information you may want to stress. To change this function, select *Edit* from the top menu bar on the main Worldox screen and then *Preferences > Worldox*. You should see two lists, similar to those shown in Figure 8.2. Under *File List Options*, scroll down and select *Column Headers Size Automatically*. Double-click on this and change the setting to *No*.

Figure 8.2 Preferences Not To Size Column Headers Automatically

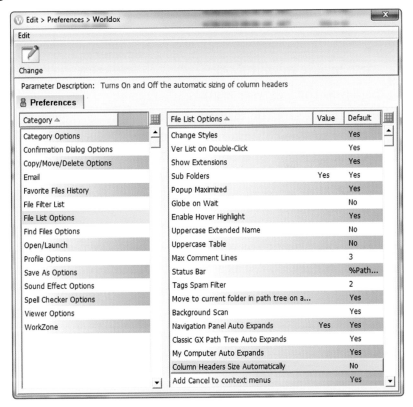

Adding Columns to the Display

You can easily add columns to the display. Simply left-click in any gray area on the column headers list (on the right-hand side in Figure 8.1). A menu of options pops up. The columns that are currently displayed are checked. You can select any additional columns for display including information other than fields in the Profile Group (see Figure 8.3).

Figure 8.3 Column Options

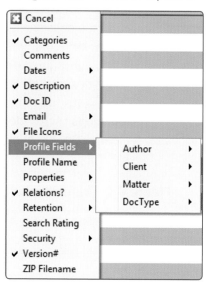

Drag the columns around until they are displayed the way you want. When you are done, save the display by right-clicking on the column headers list and selecting **Save Column Template**. Give it a name so it appears next time you open Worldox, and choose a descriptive name so you can easily find it.

You can have different displays for different functions. For example, you might want to have an e-mail display that shows the To and From fields from e-mails. You might want to have a display that can be customized for export to Excel to use as a table of contents for a real estate binder, a list of exhibits for a trial, a list for document production, a privileged document log, or some other kind of table of contents. You can save multiple templates and recall them later to use as the basis for other displays.

Worldox Window Styles

You can customize and save all the various options that make up the overall display of the Worldox screen, including the navigation pane and the Forms bar at the bottom of the Worldox window. This is also the best way to save the initial display when Worldox opens. Worldox refers to this overall customization as a Window Style. To save a Window Style, click on the blue diskette icon (see Figure 8.4) at just above and to the right of the column headers on the file list.

Figure 8.4 Save Window Style Icon

Figure 8.5 Window Style Options

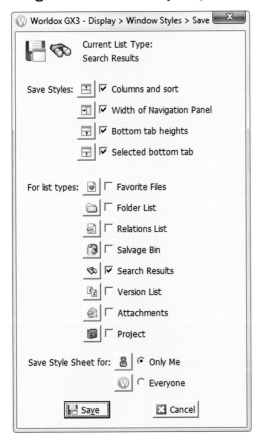

A dialog box appears, showing the options you can select to display as the default (Figure 8.5). These combine any default options that have not been changed with any specific customizations you have made. Choose the options that you want and then click **Save**.

You can save only one style for each Search Template. In addition, you must save a separate style for each Search Template, or you will get unexpected results when you execute a search.

Creating Bookmarks

Bookmarks are one of the most valuable tools in managing Worldox. They are similar to shortcuts or bookmarks in a browser: they take you directly to the places you want to go. You can use Worldox bookmarks as "rolling searches." If there is an active case you want to search regularly, you can create a bookmark for it. When the case is over, you can delete the bookmark by right-clicking on it and selecting *Delete Bookmark*.

There are two kinds of bookmarks: search based and directory based. Here's how to create them.

Search-Based Bookmarks

First, do the search that you want to use as the basis for a bookmark. For example, search for all the files listed under a given client or matter.

When the search completes, if you already have a bookmark bar (see Lesson 3, Figure 3.7 for an example), right-click on it and select *Add this list*. Otherwise, go to **Bookmarks** on the top menu bar and select *Add this list*. At this point, a pop-up box gives you two options, as shown in Figure 8.6.

1. **Perform Search** or **Show Template**. If you want the bookmark to actually do the search, select *Perform Search*. When you click on the bookmark, the search will be performed. These searches are dynamic: if you add more files that satisfy the criteria, they come up automatically every time you do the search.

   Show Template opens the search with criteria partially filled in. You might want to use this for a search where you want to add criteria to those defined in the search. For example, I have an e-mail search defined that pre-fills the "e-mail" document type. I can then add a sender, recipient, or client to the search. You could also set a bookmark for Westlaw or LexisNexis decisions profiled to a general research location so you can easily search case law you might have saved.

Figure 8.6 Create Bookmark Optioins

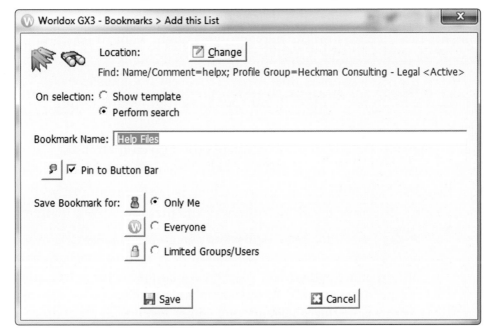

2. **Pin to Button Bar**. This puts the search on the button bar. There is a finite amount of real estate to hold bookmarks. You can have up to five rows. If you do not select **Pin to Button Bar**, the bookmark will still show up in the navigation pane on the left side of the Worldox screen. Search bookmarks have a binoculars icon on the bookmark bar.

Directory-Based Bookmarks

These are bookmarks that point to a specific directory. To create a directory bookmark, scroll down to that directory in the navigation pane. The contents of the directory will appear in the Worldox main screen. Create the bookmark in the same way you would create a search-based bookmark.

Directory bookmarks are much more limited than search bookmarks but can be useful in certain cases. For example, if you typically scan documents to a directory on the network, you might want to set up a bookmark to that directory rather than having to locate it every time you need to process a scanned document. Directory bookmarks have a file folder icon on the bookmark bar (See Lesson 3, Figure 3.7 for an example).

But if you want to find all the documents for a given matter, for example, a search is much more efficient. Also, if your system is configured so that the Doc Type field is a directory (which is fairly common), you cannot create a directory search that finds all the files for a given matter.

NOTE If you have Managerial rights, you can create a bookmark for the entire firm or for a selected group of people (a practice area, for example). Otherwise, you can e-mail the bookmark to other users. This process is the same as e-mailing Quick Profiles: right-click on the bookmark and select **Email to another user**.

TIP Bookmarks sort alphabetically. If you want to manually place certain bookmarks first, include a period at the beginning of the names. This will cause them to sort first. For more elaborate sorting, you could group bookmarks by different punctuation, such as a period or a hyphen. Thus you might have three sets of bookmarks, each sorted alphabetically internally: the first starting with a period, the second starting with no punctuation, and the third starting with a hyphen. But remember, generally speaking, less is more.

TIP You can create a bookmark for all those shortcuts you copied from your desktop using WorkZone (see Lesson 4). When you copy them, include some unique set of characters in the Description or Comments field, such as *zzz*. Then create a search for all files with *zzz* in the description and a bookmark for the results. Low-tech but very effective. See Lesson 3, Figure 3.7, for a sample bookmark bar.

Creating a Search Template

You may want several search templates for different functions; for example, a standard search template for documents (Figure 8.7) and an e-mail search template (Figure 8.8).

Figure 8.7 Standard Search Template

Figure 8.8 E-mail Search Template

| NOTE | These templates are a bit different from what Worldox installs by default. I put the Name/Comment and Text in File fields at the top, next to each other, because I find that more efficient. For most firms, Date Modified is an adequate search, and the template does not have to be cluttered with other date options. Note also that the e-mail template has added fields for e-mail addresses and "EMAIL" is already filled in for DocType. |

To create a search template, click the ***Options*** button at the bottom of an existing template and then choose ***Customize Fields***. You can add, subtract, or reposition fields. When you are done, click ***OK***. Then click ***Options*** again and select ***Save Template***. Be sure to give the template a new name; otherwise, it will overwrite your existing template and can be somewhat onerous to undo.

If you need to search multiple profile groups regularly (legacy and client files, for example), you can create a search template to do that. After you click on ***Options***, select the profile groups you want to search and save the template as, for example, "Legacy and Client" or some similar name. Note that when searching multiple profile groups, you can search only fields that are common to all groups.

Associating a Bookmark with a Search Template

You can associate different search templates with different column displays (for example, for e-mail). This is not difficult but depends on performing a number of steps in a precise order.

1. First, as described above, create the search template you want to use and save it.

2. Do a blank search (i.e., with no information in any field unless you want it to appear every single time you do this search) based on the template you have created. This is essential: any information you might put in this search will be incorporated into the final bookmark. Note that if you are creating a base template for all searches, this "search" may warn that it will return thousands or even hundreds of thousands of results. That is correct. You have to do this search to associate the template with the bookmark.

3. With the search results on the screen, create your column display. Save this display as a column template first (give it a name) so that you can recall it if you need to fix anything in the future.

4. Save the display again. This time, save it as the default for this search template. Do *not* make any changes to the Template Name field (see the example in Figure 8.9).

5. Add the bookmark to the bookmark bar. Every time you do a search using this bookmark, the columns you specified for just that search will display.

Figure 8.9 Save Column Template Screen

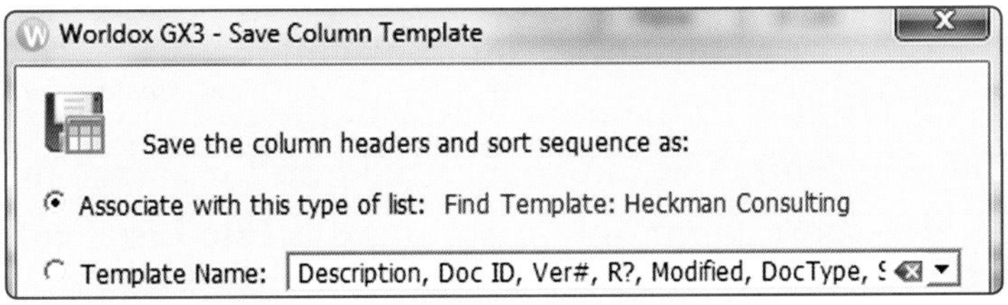

Worldox GX3 - Save Column Template

Save the column headers and sort sequence as:

⊙ Associate with this type of list: Find Template: Heckman Consulting

○ Template Name: | Description, Doc ID, Ver#, R?, Modified, DocType, S ▾

Customizing the Button Bar

You can also customize the button bar at the top of the main screen. To change an individual button, simply right-click on it and select the desired option from the menu (shown in Figure 8.10). You can change the appearance of the button (icon or text), move it left or right, or add another button.

You can also customize the way the entire bar appears. Right-click in an empty space to the right of your existing buttons. Click any of the right-pointing arrows (see Figure 8.11) and select additional buttons to display.

Figure 8.10
Customize Button

Figure 8.11
Customize Entire Button Bar

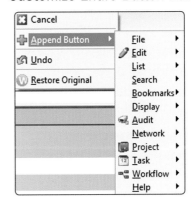

Customizing the Display Screen

You can also customize many options in the Worldox main screen. To do this, click on ***Display*** in the top menu bar, then choose ***Appearance*** and select ***Color*** or ***Font***. You can change the font for a large number of display items. The most commonly customized is **File List Profiles**, which is the main display screen. As monitors get larger, your text may look smaller. You may want to make the display text a large point size for easier reading. Of course, this reduces the amount of text you can display, so you will need to find a trade-off you are comfortable with.

You can also customize the color of the bookmarks bar to make it stand out more. I usually make it light yellow, and many of my clients simply refer to it as "the yellow bar." Select the ***Bookmark Button Bar*** option under ***Display > Appearance > Colors > Colors***.

Figure 8.12 Customize Line Colors

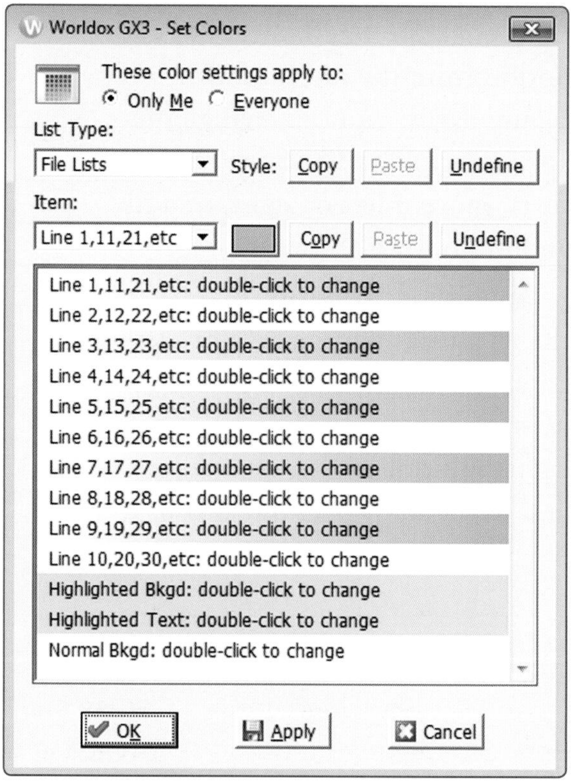

You can similarly customize other colors. By default, Worldox makes alternating lines of the display a light gray for ease of reading. If you want, you can change this to some other color. Under ***Display> Appearance> Colors*** choose ***File Lists***. The box shown in Figure 8.12 will appear.

For example, to change the alternate line colors in Figure 8.1, you would do the following: ***Ctrl + right-click*** on the column header row and pick the color to display on lines 1, 11, 21, and so on. Then click the ***Copy*** button. Go to the third row and paste for lines 3, 13, 23, and so on. Repeat for rows 5, 7, and 9. Click ***OK*** when you are done.

By default, when you sort documents in descending order by Date Modified, Worldox displays an Outlook-style notification telling you when documents were last changed. Since the documents are in descending order, I usually get rid of the Outlook-style display to show more documents (since the sort order is the same in either case). To do this, right-click on the column header **Modified** and select ***Hide Groupings***. If you right-click on it a second time, you can choose ***Show Groupings***.

There are a number of other options under the **Display** menu that enable you to show or hide various options. Those who prefer a "leaner" display may choose to hide options they rarely use. I generally don't recommend this, because when the day comes that you *do* want a particular option, you may not readily recall how to re-display it.

Navigation Pane

The navigation pane displays on the left side of the Worldox main screen. It can be turned on or off with the **Navigation Pane** button on the button bar (typically the second or third button from the right) or ***Ctrl + T***. As with most Windows applications, you can permanently size this pane. However, when you hover the mouse over the pane, it expands temporarily to make the contents easier to read, so you can have a narrow column for ordinary use and a wider one when you need it. This is especially useful if you are scrolling up and down a directory structure.

You can set which options display on the navigation pane and in what order by clicking on the small wrench at the bottom. Icons for any options that have been hidden show next to the wrench. When you click on the wrench, a menu will let you check or uncheck items to display and move the order up or down.

As we have learned in this lesson, customizing Worldox can help you better work the way you want. In the next lesson you will learn how to organize your documents in ways that go beyond the basic Profile Group operations and which can provide significant addition options.

Related Documents, Categories, Projects, Workspaces

Worldox has four functions that might be called metadata functions; that is, ways of organizing information over and above the fields provided by the profile groups and data that Worldox tracks by default, such as Date Modified. These include Relations (related documents), Categories, Projects, and Workspaces. To a large extent, these are different ways to accomplish the same thing: organizing and relating files that are otherwise unrelated in Worldox. They provide the basis for a "table of contents" that lists the various files together.

Relations

Related documents follow a parent-child logic. Suppose you have one of the following lists: closing documents, exhibits for a trial, or various files and e-mails that are related to one portion of a case. You can make your main document—a table of contents, for example—the "parent." Then the documents in the list become "children." (You can also set up a multilayer system with grandchildren, which appear as the children's children.)

Relating two documents is extremely easy. Click on the child-to-be and drag it on top of the parent-to-be. You will be asked if you want to relate the documents. Click **Yes**. It's that simple.

To view all the relations of a document, select the document and then click the **Relations** button on the button bar or the **Relations** tab at the bottom of the main screen. **Alt + Ctrl + R** also lists the relations for a document.

If you make a mistake and need to "unrelate" a document, first select the parent. Then, at the bottom of the screen, click on the **Relations** tab. Choose the document to be removed and click **Remove Relation**.

NOTE	You have to remove the child relations one at a time, and you cannot remove a parent relation.

Once you are done, you might have a list similar to Figure 9.1. The table of contents of this book is the parent to eleven child documents (thus the P11 designation), and each child document has one parent.

Figure 9.1 Parent-Child Listing

	Description	Doc ID	Ver#	R? △		Modified	DocType
	One Hour ch. 6 Quick Profiles	00020143.WPD			C1	5/4/2013 08:34 AM	ART
	One Hour ch. 5 Outlook Integration	00020142.WPD			C1	5/4/2013 08:24 AM	ART
	One Hour ch. 4 Getting Legacy documents into Worldox	00020133.WPD			C1	5/3/2013 03:57 PM	ART
	One Hour Ch. 3 Searching and Finding	00020111.WPD			C1	5/3/2013 11:44 AM	ART
	One Hour Ch. 2 Saving Documents	00020105.WPD			C1	5/3/2013 10:11 AM	ART
	One Hour: Ch 1: Considerations in Configuring Worldox	00020102.WPD			C1	5/3/2013 08:46 AM	ART
	one hour ch 10 Trouble-shooting Worldox	00020181.WPD			C1	5/2/2013 09:36 AM	ART
	one hour ch 9 Productivity Suite	00020180.WPD			C1	5/1/2013 01:28 PM	ART
	One Hour ch. 7 Customizing Worldox	00020172.WPD			C1	4/30/2013 02:50 PM	ART
	One Hour - Introduction	00020097.WPD			C1	4/30/2013 02:44 PM	ART
	one hour ch 8 metadata	00020179.WPD			C1	4/30/2013 02:35 PM	ART
	One Hour Table of Contents	00020108.WPD			P11	4/29/2013 02:50 PM	ART

When you create a new document, you may want to relate it to an existing document. When you save the file, click on the **Relations** menu button (see Figure 9.2) at the top of the File Save form.

Figure 9.2 Relations Menu on Save Profile Screen

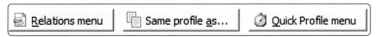

Then select ***Relate this file to***. The Worldox file list will pop up, and you can select or search for the file to which this file is to be related. It will become a child of the file you select.

 NOTE When you display the contents of related files, versions, or projects, it may be somewhat unclear how you return to the previous display. You can click on the **Home** button (the house icon) to display your saved favorites. Alternatively, the previous search/sort is displayed above the Location bar just below the bookmark bar. In the example shown in Figure 9.3 below, you would click on **Book** to return from the display of related files.

Figure 9.3 Return to Previous Screen

Categories

A very common request from Worldox users is for the ability to assign a document to more than one matter or document type. The new Categories feature gives you an equivalent of this functionality. To create a new Category, right-click in the blank area of the **Categories** column in the file list on the main screen and select ***Add/Edit Categories***. You will see the box shown in Figure 9.4.

To add a new category, click on **Add** (green plus sign). You will be asked to select the type of category (your own personal category or one based on a specific folder), name the category, and select an icon that will be associated with it. When you associate multiple categories with a file and there is not sufficient room to display all the names, only the icons are displayed, so it would be wise to put some thought into the icon. Worldox offers over two hundred icons that can be associated with categories. A small sample is shown in Figure 9.5:

Figure 9.4 Category Menu

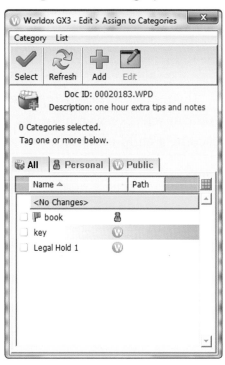

Figure 9.5
Some Category Icons

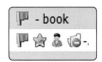

BEST PRACTICE Firms should select a set of default public categories that are standardized across the firm. This will prevent the creation of duplicate categories that may have slightly different names but are, in fact, the same thing. Individual users can then create their own categories as well. To use categories efficiently, the firm should first make sure that there is a Categories column in the file list and a **Categories** button on the button bar.

<table>
<tr><td>

NOTE

</td><td>

You can associate multiple files with one category in a batch, but only from the Categories column. If you click on the **Categories** button, you can associate only one file at a time with a given category. You can however, associate multiple categories with the same file at one time.

The firm can set Categories to be more or less intrusive, depending on its workflow. Categories can be set to pop up as an option every time you save, open, copy, or move a file, which is helpful if you use categories extensively and/or want to enforce use. Alternatively, the function can be set so that users must assign categories manually.

At present (mid-2013), it is not possible to search for categories. However, this functionality is under development.

</td></tr>
</table>

Projects

The Project function offers a way to group documents together, similar to Relations. The difference is that a Worldox Project exists as a separate document with "pointers" to the files it contains. You can drag and drop files to a project. Usually there is a separate profile group called Workspace or Projects, organized by user or client. Once the firm has created this profile group, end users can create their own projects.

Projects are typically used to gather together documents that might not otherwise be associated. You can think of projects as "virtual folders" in which to store documents. They serve to categorize files the same way a folder would. Some examples would be

- real estate closing binders;
- lists of exhibits in a trial;
- all the firm's manuals, handbooks, and help documentation (for Worldox, for example), which users can then see at a glance;

- forms for various types of law; and
- electronic court filings for federal litigation.

There are two ways to create projects. The classic way uses the **Project** tab on the bar at the bottom of the Worldox main screen.

Figure 9.6 Project Document Selection Screen

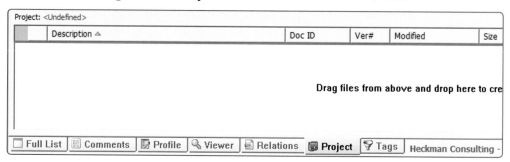

When you click the *Project* tab, a window opens up, similar to the one shown in Figure 9.6. Select the files you want to include in the project and drag and drop them into the project window. Once this is done, click *Save As* in the menu at the right of the window (see Figure 9.7 below). Select the project profile group and give the project a name, just as you do when you are saving a document.

You can also use this menu to add more files or remove a file.

Figure 9.7
Projects Menu

NOTE You must select **Close** to close the project window; it does not close automatically.

Projects have a WDL extension and can be searched for, the same as regular documents.

Projects and Workspaces

Once you have created a project or two, the easiest way to manage them is through Workspaces in the navigation pane.

To select and use projects, open ***Workspaces***. Right-click on ***My Workspaces*** and choose ***Subscribe to*** for the appropriate directory or profile group, probably Projects (see Figure 9.8). A list of possible users or matters will pop up and you subscribe to the one you want.

Figure 9.8 Subscribing to Projects

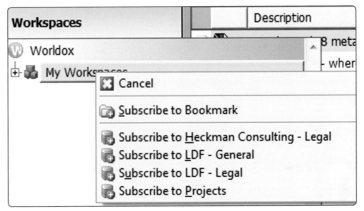

At that point, you can create a new project simply by right-clicking on the subscribed folder, selecting ***Create Project***, and giving it a name. Then you can drag and drop files to the desired project.

NOTE	Projects are directory based. The files that make up a project must all reside in the same directory; they cannot be based on search criteria grouping, such as all documents of a given type, regardless of what matter they belong to. Projects must be created and managed manually. That said, they offer an excellent way of organizing files that might otherwise be located under disparate clients or topics.

Productivity Suite

For most of its twenty-five-year existence, Worldox limited itself to providing the best document management features possible and focused on integrating with other products to increase functionality. More recently, it has begun including additional features, such as document retention or legal holds. The Productivity Suite contains modules (available at extra cost) that add significant additional functionality, in response to frequent requests from users. There are six modules:

- **Workflow** enables automated reviews, approvals, and transmittals for documents in Worldox.

- **Task** lets you schedule Outlook reminders for specific documents.

- **Notify** lets users receive e-mail notifications when specified actions are taken on particular files or folders.

- **Chat** is an in-house instant messaging application for Worldox users.

- **compareDocs** allows document comparison of most file types (except PDF to PDF).

- **pdfDocs** is a PDF generator with many security features.

Both compareDocs and pdfDocs are available through Worldox only for sites with twenty-five or fewer users.

Workflow

Workflow is by far the most significant feature of the Productivity Suite. It lets you route one or more documents to one or more users for consideration or approval. You can also create multiple routes so that the second route is engaged only if the document is approved in the first route.

First select the document(s) to be routed, then click on the ***Create*** button for Workflow on your button bar or select ***Workflow > Create*** from the top menu. (If there is no Create button and you will be using this feature frequently, consider adding one to your button bar. See Lesson 8 for instructions.) A dialog box pops up, similar to the one shown in Figure 10.1.

Figure 10.1 Workflow Creation Screen

The procedure should be fairly self-explanatory:

- Fill in the subject line (this is like the subject line in Outlook).

- Put in any message you want the recipient(s) to receive.

- Click the **Question** button. A pop-up box will give you three options, as shown in Figure 10.2: **Review/Comment**, **Approve/Reject**, and **Rate from 1-5**. Select the appropriate option.

- Click the **Route is a** button and give the criteria that will make the route a success (see Figure 10.3).

Figure 10.2
Workflow Question Options

Figure 10.3 Workflow Success Options

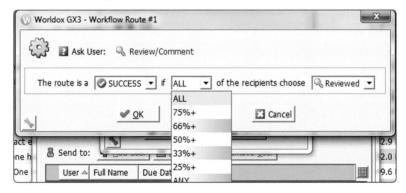

- Click the **Due Date** button and give the date and time. There are default options for **Today** and **Tomorrow**, or you can set a custom date and time.

- Select the recipients for Route 1.

Repeat as needed for multiple routes. If you have multiple routes, you can have different messages for each route. If you select only one route, the message is broadcast to all recipients. For multiple routes, the first route must be completed successfully before proceeding to the second route. This can be useful for processes that may require multiple approvals, such as expense reports that might have to be approved by a department head before being forwarded to accounting for payment.

Reviewing and Managing Workflows

Once you have sent out a workflow, it appears below the document in question, like a comment (see the example in Figure 10.4).

Figure 10.4 Workflow Status

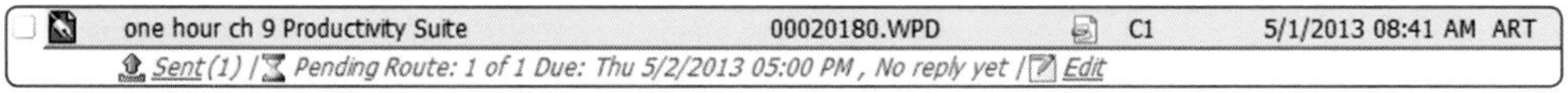

This lets you see who has responded to the workflow (in the above example, there is no reply yet). You can edit the options from here by clicking on **Edit**.

When you click on **Sent** (see Figure 10.4), a workflow window similar to the one in Figure 10.5 appears.

When you select a given workflow, you see the status and the amount of time until it is due in the second and third sections of the window.

You can also manage all your workflows centrally from the navigation pane.

Figure 10.5 Workflow Details

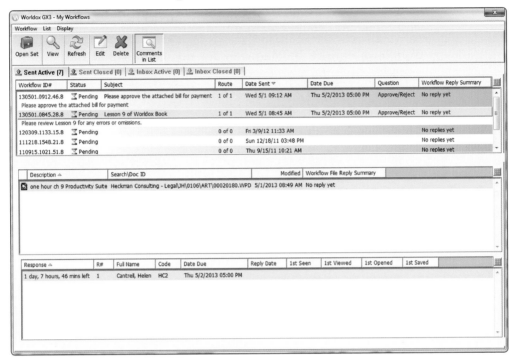

Workflow Templates

If you have workflows that you use all the time (for bill or expense report approvals, for example), you can make templates that predefine those workflows.

Select ***Workflow > Template*** from the menu to create and save a workflow template. The only difference between a template and a specific workflow is that the due date in a template is defined as a certain number of hours or days after the workflow has been sent.

Save the template and give it a name.

TIP	If you routinely scan incoming e-mail, you might want to create templates to route all the scans to any lawyers who need to review them. You could create a template for each lawyer.
NOTE	Workflows can be defined only for documents that have been profiled within the Worldox system.

Task

The Task function creates a reminder in Outlook. When you select **Task > Create** from the Worldox menu, you get the dialog box shown in Figure 10.6:

Figure 10.6 Task Creation

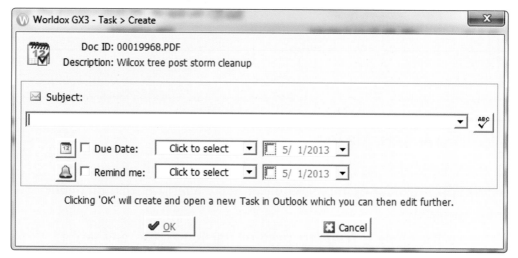

This is pretty self-explanatory. Once the task is created in Worldox, it appears in Outlook and you can manage it there.

Notify

Worldox tracks over thirty different file operations (for example: opening, saving, copying, renaming, moving, and downloading files; checking documents in and out) and produces an audit trail of these operations. The Notify function lets you set "rules" to alert users via e-mail whenever one or more of the audit trail actions has been taken on specific documents, matters, or other files.

To start a rule, select *Audit > Notify* on the main menu. Click the green plus sign to add a new rule. This opens the dialog box shown in Figure 10.7. (If you have rules that have already been created, they will appear at the left.)

Figure 10.7 Notify Options

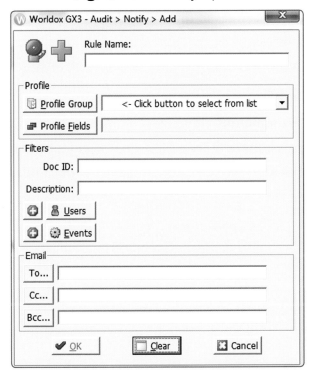

This dialog is fairly self-explanatory:

- Give the rule a name.

- Select the profile group the rule should draw information from. When the group pops up, if you want the rule to apply to a specific client, matter, or other item, select that information.

- If you want the rule to apply to a specific file, type in the full document ID (including leading zeros). There is no lookup available in this field; you must know the ID.

- If you want the rule to apply to files with specific text in the description, input that text. If you want to target an exact phrase, put it in quotation marks; for example, "executed contract."

- Click on **Users** and **Events** to select specific users and events to be monitored. For example, if you want to monitor when a certain document has been saved or renamed, you would select those Event options.

- Select the users to be notified when the monitored events occur.

When the rule has been saved, it appears when you select **Audit > Notify** from the main menu.

You can also search for activity monitored by any of the rules you have set up. Select **Audit > Notify** and the rule you wish to monitor. Then click on the binoculars icon in the toolbar.

Chat

Chat is an in-house instant messaging system. It pops up in the lower right-hand corner of your screen. However, Chat does not function in a Citrix or Terminal Server remote access session, so users connected using these services would not be able to chat with the normal network users and vice-versa. In addition, many firms have in-house IM services via various practice management programs. Chat is turned off by default. Tech support can turn it on.

compareDocs

The compareDocs feature is installed to the default Worldox document comparison function. When you click on the **Compare** button, compareDocs is used automatically if it has been installed. See Advanced Topics for information on using the comparison function.

The compareDocs menu, shown in Figure 10.8, offers a number of options.

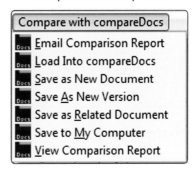

Figure 10.8
CompareDocs Options

pdfDocs

The pdfDocs function is a full-fledged alternative to Acrobat. It is focused on creating binders and organizing your PDF documents. It also greatly facilitates publishing documents in PDF/A format. You can import documents from Worldox, process them with pdfDocs, and save them back. A sample pdfDocs window is shown in Figure 10.9.

Figure 10.9 pdfDocs Showing Import from Worldox

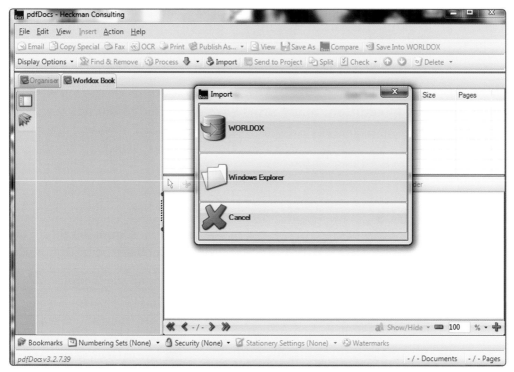

The simplest way to create a PDF version of a Word document when pdfDocs is installed is to right-click on the document in the file list on the Worldox main screen and select ***Send To > (pdfDocs) Create as New Document*** or ***Send To > (pdfDocs) Email as PDF***. A more complete review of the program's functionality is beyond the scope of this book.

As with any software program, you may occasionally experience difficulties in the day to day operation of Worldox. The next lesson addresses some common problems and how best to deal with them short of calling on your IT department or consultant.

Troubleshooting Worldox

For most problems with Worldox that need assistance or troubleshooting, you should check with your IT department or consultant or contact Worldox tech support. In this lesson, we'll start with how to handle indexing issues, which are the most common problems firms are likely to encounter with Worldox but the easiest to remedy.

When you have a problem with Worldox (or any other software), it is useful to have some idea of what the cause might be and be able to give a good description of the issue to a tech support person. After all, if you take your car to the garage, you need to be able to give the mechanic more information than "my car doesn't work." Consequently, this lesson is organized by problem.

I Can't Find My Documents

There are variants of this, such as "Search is not working" or "Document *x* has disappeared." The problem is sometimes combined with the fact that documents appear on your most recently used list but a search does not find them.

In the vast majority of cases, this symptom is due to a problem with the dedicated PC used to maintain and update Worldox indexes (known as the Indexer). You should report the first instance of a search not working, rather than waiting. I have seen firms where when the problem was finally reported, the Indexer had been nonoperational for several days.

If you believe a failed search is related to Indexer issues, repeat a search that you know has worked in the past to see whether it works. If it does, the problem may just be user error in formulating the search.

BEST PRACTICE	It is highly desirable for a firm to designate a fairly tech-savvy user, paralegal, or office manager to have remote access to the Indexer from his or her own desktop. Then, as soon as the first person reports a search failure, the designee can log into the Indexer and fix the issue if it is relatively simple.
NOTE	Indexer errors are usually caused by a variety of issues unrelated to the Worldox program itself, most commonly having to do with network connectivity, failure to turn off automatic updates, or network updates running at night that break the connection with the Indexer.

Along "is it plugged in" lines, if the Indexer is just sitting there and has not been logged in to, log in. It should start automatically.

Figure 11.1 shows the basic Indexer screen.

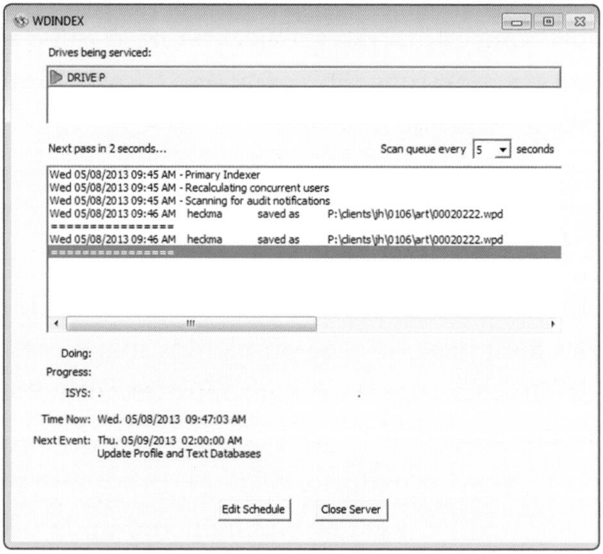

If you don't see an active countdown (*Next pass in 10 seconds . . . 9 seconds . . . 8 seconds*), then the indexer is "hung." You may also see

Figure 11.1 Main Indexer Screen

one or more error messages. Dismiss these. Then click *Close Server* and *Agree* to confirm closing. Select the drive letters to be indexed. Then, in the top menu (Figure 11.2), click *Server* > *Start*.

Figure 11.2 Indexer Menu Options

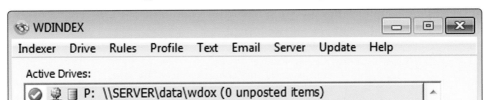

The Indexer should start up again and begin processing all the files that previously "could not be found" when doing searches. If you see dozens of files start to scroll by, the problem has been fixed, and users should be able to search again.

If there is a message that the Indexer is busy, there are two copies of it trying to run. Exit all instances of the Indexer (you may have to use Task Manager to do this) and restart it. If the busy message persists, contact your network IT person (in some cases, multiple users may be logged in to the Indexer).

If this does not fix the problem, the indexes may be off-line. (One indication of this is that end users may get a message that the indexes are off-line.) Stop the Indexer as above. Then click on a drive letter and select *Profile*, then *Properties*. At the bottom of the window, in the *Current Status* box, make sure *On-line – ready to find by Profile* is checked. Repeat for **Text** and **Properties**. Do this for each drive letter.

Worldox Won't Start or Says It Is "Off-Line"

If Worldox won't start or says it is off-line, then your PC is not connected to the network properly. You will see the message shown in Figure 11.3 when Worldox opens:

Figure 11.3 Off-Line Message

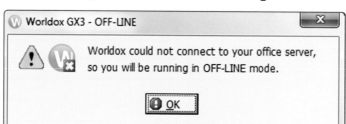

In addition, the Worldox icon in the system tray will look like this: Reboot your PC or contact your IT person.

The Worldox Screen Is Blank When I Open It

A common reason for this is that your PC is not logged into the network properly. Check for a red *X* on the Worldox icon in the system tray (see icon above). If you see it, Worldox is not connected to the network. There are two steps you can take that might remedy this situation; if they do not work, contact your IT people.

1. Simply log off and log back in again (you don't need to fully reboot your PC) to see if the problem resolves itself.

2. Open Windows Explorer and navigate to the drive letter where your documents are stored. Click on the drive letter to see the directories. If you initially see a red *X* (Figure 11.4) but when you click on the drive letter the directory displays correctly, restart Worldox.

The issue here may be that for some reason the login script that connects users to the network is not functioning properly or needs to be adjusted.

Figure 11.4 Drives Offline

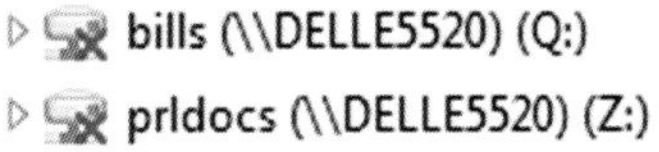

▷ 🖥 bills (\\DELLE5520) (Q:)
▷ 🖥 prldocs (\\DELLE5520) (Z:)

Documents Are in the Format JH001234.doc

In this case, Worldox has not been able to connect to the network properly and/or users do not have proper permissions (all users need full control of the files in the Worldox program directory). Users may have created documents off-line without even realizing it. These documents will have to be checked in.

Legacy Documents Cannot Be Viewed or Moved to Worldox

Scroll to any directory in your legacy documents folder. Files should be displayed in the Doc ID column in the format *docume~1.doc*. If the Doc ID column is blank or files are displayed in some other format (sometimes a name starting with a bar, such as *|PFXYZ.doc*), there is a serious problem with your document store, having to do with what is known as "8.3 support." You need to report this to your IT department or consultant.

The Document No Longer Exists

If Worldox says that a document no longer exists, it might have been moved. You may be able to find it using the audit trail described below in Mysterious Happenings.

Document Has Been Deleted

If a document has been deleted, the firm's Worldox Manager should be able to retrieve it from the Salvage Bin. If you have the rights to do this, you will see **Salvage** displayed under your profile in the navigation pane, as shown in Figure 11.5.

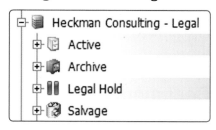

Figure 11.5 Salvage Bin

You can search the Salvage Bin by clicking on the ***Search What?*** button at the bottom of a search dialog box and selecting ***Salvage Bin***.

Mysterious Happenings

When something mysterious has happened to a document, one of the first things to do is run an audit query. You can run an audit query by right-clicking on the document and selecting ***Audit > File***. This will show you everything that has happened to the document.

Assuming you have the rights, you can also run a more systematic audit trail; for example, for a "missing" document. To do this, select ***Audit > Search*** from

Figure 11.6 Audit Trail Query

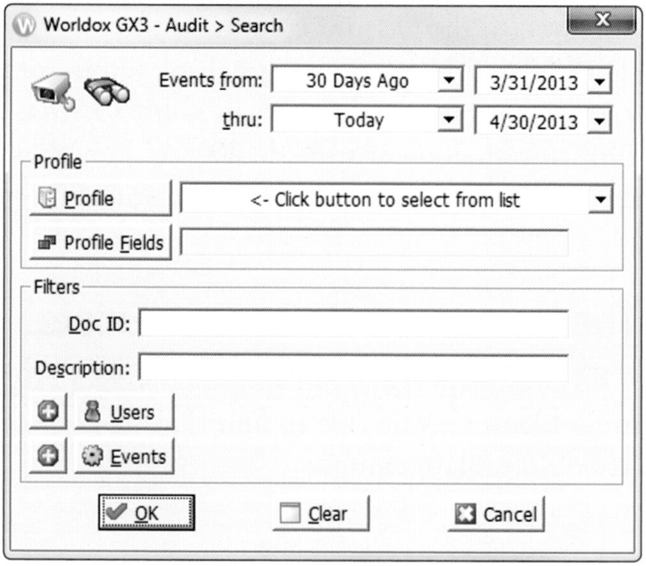

the main menu (or ***Ctrl + F7***). A dialog box similar to the one in Figure 11.6 will pop up.

Fill in the information you are searching for. You must select a profile. You can select a specific user and specific events (for example, moved or deleted) if desired. Click ***OK*** to run the report. This will give you a report on all activity that satisfies your criteria.

The Red *X* Is Disabled: I Can't Exit Out of Word

By default, the red *X* in the upper right corner of a Word or WordPerfect screen is disabled by Worldox. The reason for this is that using it prevents Worldox from auditing File Close events properly. In certain infrequent circumstances, it can also lead to data loss.

There are two alternative ways of exiting Word: First, you can use the standard Windows keystroke for closing programs: ***Alt + F4***. Second, if you customize the Quick Access toolbar in Word, you can put the **Exit** command on it, which appears as a large *X* (see Figure 11.7), along with other useful operations, such as creating a new document, opening a file, or ***Save*** or ***Save As***.

Figure 11.7 "X" to Exit Word

The Worldox button bar for WordPerfect includes an exit-door icon toward the right of the bar that closes WordPerfect.

Can I Disable the Footer in Word?

There are a number of Worldox actions that can be performed on Word documents. When you click on the Worldox menu item in Word, you will see the ribbon bar of options shown in Figure 11.8.

Figure 11.8 Worldox Options in Word 2010

In particular, see at the left *Update Footer*, *Clear Whole Stamp*, and *Clear Stamp code*.

Conflicts with Keystroke Shortcuts

In certain unusual cases, the keystroke shortcut implemented for Windows by some other program can conflict with the Worldox keystroke shortcut. If you get unexpected results, this will have to be looked at on a case-by-case basis by tech support. Using the iTunes Outlook add-in on your PC can cause problems with the Worldox-Outlook integration, for example. (But should anybody be running iTunes at work?)

In the next and last lesson we will consider some advanced topics which may not be of use to everyone, but will be extremely useful to those who wish to avail themselves of these topics.

Advanced Topics

Worldox Managers are those users who are able to make changes to settings that affect the firm as a whole, such as standard bookmarks or Quick Profiles. Anytime you see a function that is labeled "Public" or "Everyone" it means that those features must be set by someone with Managerial rights. While most Managerial options are beyond the scope of this book, it is useful to know that they exist so that the firm can customize Worldox to best fit the way it works.

Most administrative functions are extremely easy to master. Typically, someone such as an office administrator will be able to perform many of them. This can be an important factor in the decision to purchase Worldox. One potential client summed it up nicely: "So you don't have to be an SQL guru to administer Worldox." Exactly. This in turn means major savings, especially for small firms that do not have the resources to hire an SQL programmer to maintain their document management system.

When Users Leave and Matters Close

Worldox licensing is based on concurrent use, which in practice means the number of users whose PCs are logged in to the network at any given moment. You can have thirty users and just twelve licenses if only twelve PCs will be on at one time.

When people leave the firm, you should not delete them from the list of users entirely. They will have documents under their names that might be "orphaned" if their user IDs were to be removed. Instead, make those users inactive.

By analogy, when a matter closes and you do not want it cluttering up your Client/Matter lists, you can mark the matter as inactive, if you have the appropriate rights. This means that the documents are all still there, but the matter no longer appears on the lists. However, any search for documents still works in an inactive matter. See Making a Client or Matter Inactive (below) for instructions.

Adding Clients and Matters

Most firms get their client/matter lists from their time and billing program. Worldox sells links to most popular SQL-based accounting programs that automatically add new client/matter numbers to Worldox when they are added to the accounting program. Smaller firms may need to add them manually, however.

BEST PRACTICE The ability to add or edit Client/Matter/DocType tables should be assigned to only a few people at a firm, not only to insure consistency and accuracy but also to prevent the creation of two or more matters with slightly different names that are, in fact, the same matter. It is imperative that this functionality be centralized.

The easiest way to add a client or matter in Worldox is to begin from a blank document in Word or WordPerfect. Start to save the document so that the File Save form appears. Click on the *Client* button and the client list pops up. If necessary, select **Client Table** (as opposed to **Client Favorites**). You will see the **Add**, **Edit**, and **Delete** buttons that are standard throughout Worldox (Figure A.1).

If you are adding a new client, you must first determine what the next client number will be. Worldox does not have a function that

Figure A.1
Add/Edit Icons

Add   Edit   Delete

automatically generates the next number. Make sure the Client code column is sorted in descending order (click to toggle if it is not), and note the next number. Then click the green plus sign. The new-client dialog box will pop up, as shown in Figure A.2.

Enter the code you noted previously and then a description. For a new client, you will obviously choose **Active**. Then click **OK**.

If you are adding a new matter, first click the **Client** button to select the client under which the matter will be listed. Then click the **Matter** button to see the existing matter list for that client. Click the green plus sign to add a matter. You will see a slightly different dialog box (Figure A.3) from the one for adding a new client:

By default, **linked to [client]** is selected. It is imperative that this not be changed; otherwise, the matter will appear under *every single* client.

To edit a client or matter description, first select the item to be edited, then click the **Edit** button and make changes.

BEST PRACTICE You can edit the description as you want, but do *not* change the client or matter number. There are ways to do this, but they are beyond the scope of this book.

Figure A.2 Add New Client

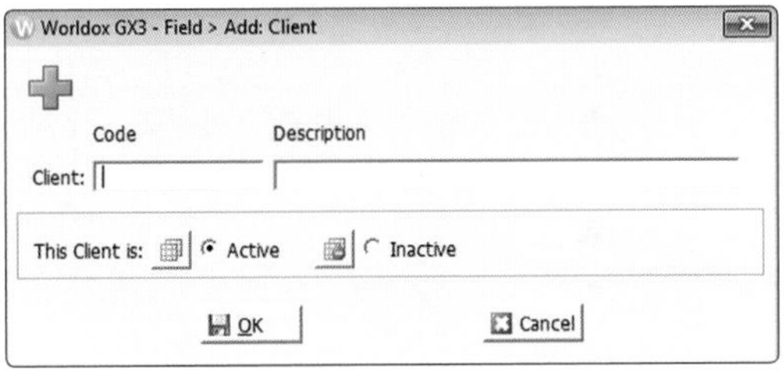

Figure A.3 Add New Matter for Existing Client

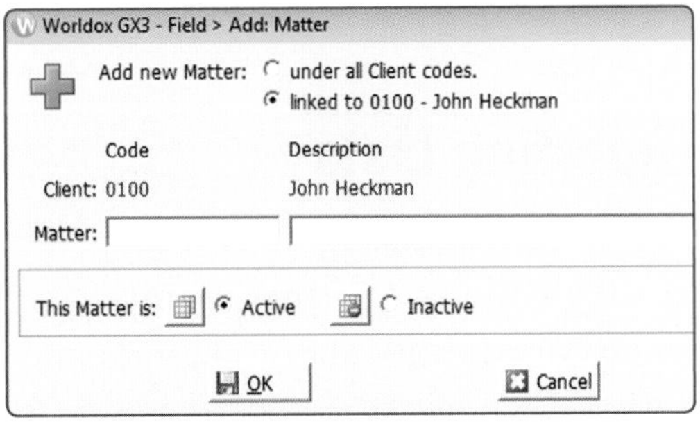

BEST PRACTICE There may be times when a lawyer has to do some work for a brand-new client immediately, and the client/matter number has not yet been entered into Worldox. The firm can create a "matter" under the Firm General client called "New matter no number yet" or something similar. That way, urgent client work gets done, and the files can be moved when the client/matter number becomes available.

Making a Client or Matter Inactive

When you edit a client or matter, you can also make it inactive by selecting the *Edit* button (see Figure A.1) and then choosing *Inactive*.

The client and matter list displays have options to let you see only active, only inactive, or both types of items, as shown in Figure A.4:

Figure A.4 Active/Inactive Buttons; Print and Export

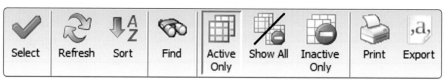

You can still search for inactive matters by selecting the *Show All* or *Inactive Only* buttons and then doing a search on the matter you need.

Exporting Lists

As you can see in Figure A.4, any Worldox list can be printed or exported to a CSV file and further manipulated from there. This can be useful if you want to think about changes and find it easier to mark up paper than to focus on a screen (I know I do). If you just want a copy of the list, select ***Print***. Otherwise, select ***Export***. Once the file has been exported and saved (not in the Worldox system), you are prompted to open it. You can then open it, print it, and save it to Worldox. When you have edited the CSV file, it can be used as the basis to reimport your changes to Worldox.

This is also helpful as the basis for any kind of table of contents, exhibits list, or privilege log.

Security and Ethical Walls

As noted in Lesson 2, end users can apply security to specific documents. An important limitation to this is that anyone with Managerial rights can override it.

Security can also be applied centrally. Managers cannot override this security (although they could, of course, change it through the administration program). Details of how to do that are outside the scope of this book, but this type of security is commonly used in the following scenarios:

- an administration profile group that only selected people have access to: typically HR, accounting, and Management Committee (In certain cases, other restricted profile groups could be created.)
- personal user "matters" so that each user has files that only he or she can access (This is somewhat more work to set up than other options for personal files, but it has some advantages.)
- ethical walls for specific clients (This is most common in areas such as sensitive mergers and acquisitions negotiations or trusts and estates work.

- in conjunction with Worldox/Web Mobile (Ethical walls can be used to give certain (usually major) clients access to selected documents. This allows Worldox to function as a limited portal for clients.)

Audit Trail

As noted in Lesson 11, the audit trail can be useful in figuring out what happened to a specific document. It can also be useful administratively to identify workloads of individual users. Further, it could conceivably be of value in terms of discovery requests.

 NOTE The red *X* to exit out of Word is disabled by default in Worldox to protect the integrity of the audit trail (see Figure 11.6). The audit trail tracks more than thirty different events but may not track your print requests.

Document Retention

Worldox includes a basic document retention function allowing you to specify that certain types of documents are to be retained for a period of time, ranging from one week to sixty-four years. For instance, a firm might want to retain correspondence for three years dating from the last time the file was modified. After that, the files can be automatically either deleted or archived by the Indexer.

One complication in this feature is that the same type of document might have to be retained for a different amount of time, depending on the type of law it is associated with. Correspondence for trusts and estates might be kept forever, for example, but correspondence for a real estate deal would only be retained for a limited period. This necessitates using an additional field in the profile group to specify the type of law, which governs how long various types of documents should be kept for that type of law.

Legal Holds

Authorized users can assign documents to Worldox's Legal Hold. Files are sent to a read-only storage location, where they can be accessed and audited (by users with the necessary rights) but cannot be edited. When appropriate, the Legal Hold can be released.

One limitation at present is that there is only *one* Legal Hold. You cannot have a Legal Hold on matter 1 and a different one on matter 2. However, by combining the Legal Hold function with Categories and assigning different holds to their respective categories, you can identify multiple Legal Holds.

Document Comparison

Worldox works with most document comparison products, including Workshare/DeltaView, compareDocs, Diff Doc, and iRedline. If the firm is using a product that does not automatically integrate, Worldox tech support can generally write the integration over the phone in a half hour or so.

To start a document comparison, select the two documents (or two versions of the document) to be compared. Then click on the *Compare* button on the Worldox button bar (or *Alt + Ctrl + C*). The document comparison dialog box comes up, similar to Figure A.5.

Figure A.5 Document Comparison Box

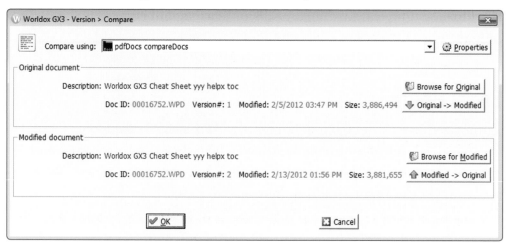

Depending on what program you are using, you will be able to set various options and complete the comparison. You can also start the process from the interface of the document comparison program.

Using the Word Document Compare Feature

For years, Microsoft has recommended against using Word's document compare feature in a legal setting, but many firms do so anyway.

To use Word's comparison feature, start from Word. When you select ***Review > Compare > Compare Documents***, the comparison dialog box (Figure A.6) pops up.

Figure A.6 Word Document Comparison Screen

You must click on the file folder icon to select documents from Worldox. If you wish to compare versions of a document, open the version list and select the desired ones.

You can select configuration options as you normally would in Word. Click **OK** to complete the comparison.

PDF Integration

Worldox does not natively convert documents to PDF. However, it does integrate with Acrobat and virtually all other PDF creation programs. If you right-click on a document in the Worldox file list and select **Send To**, you will see the various programs you can use to create PDF files.

To the extent that the PDF files have been run through optical character recognition (OCR) so that they are text searchable, Worldox full-text indexes them. If they are image-only, they cannot be indexed. In addition, Worldox does not index any document that has been given a password; it does not try to do an end run around any security that may have been set.

Scanning, Worldox, and OCR

Many firms currently scan either to a network directory or to end users' e-mail. Users must then manually move the files into Worldox. All too often, the scan directory winds up just being a dumping ground.

Worldox integrates out of the box with the Fujitsu ScanSnap line of scanners at no additional cost. These desktop scanners are excellent for relatively small volumes, such as incoming e-mail.

For larger volumes, such as briefs or discovery documents, multifunction copiers or scanners are usually the choice. Most major copier makers offer integration modules for Worldox at an additional per-copier charge (count on an initial cost of $1,500 to $2,000 per copier). Products include Sharp's SimplifyScan, Ricoh's DigiDocFlow, Xerox's ScanFlowStore, Konica Minolta's Dispatcher Phoenix, and others. In addition, copier capture programs from Equitrac, Copitrak, nQueue Billback, and eCopy also have integration modules with Worldox.

Once a document has been scanned, it must be run through Optical Caracter Recognition (OCR) to make it searchable. OCR is the most time-intensive aspect of scanning. You should count on 2.5 to 3 seconds per page, or 4 to 5 minutes of "wait time" for a hundred-page scan.

Major OCR/PDF products from companies such as Nuance and Abbyy can set "watch" directories so that OCR happens in the background after files are scanned. However, those products do not integrate directly with Worldox. A program called Symphony, from Trumpet Inc., enables documents to be OCR'd in the background with Worldox (see below).

Worldox Connectors and Third-Party Add-ins

Most major time and billing and practice management programs offer integration with Worldox, to varying degrees of adequacy.

Worldox provides "connectors" at an additional cost for most major SQL-based time and billing programs, including Elite, Omega, Orion, Juris, Tabs, ProLaw, and PCLaw (if you are running the SQL version).

A SharePoint connector was released in 2013. It allows a single instance of a document across the programs. Citrix ShareFile integration establishes a direct connection between Worldox and the ShareFile system, which eliminates the need to access ShareFile via a web interface.

Practice management programs such as Amicus, LawBase, Needles, PracticeMaster, and Time Matters also integrate with Worldox. Most often, this integration is in the form of a simple client/matter lookup.

Thus for a matter with a large number of files, this integration is only a starting point: you will probably have to refine your search once you are in Worldox. PracticeMaster is the only program that offers a full Worldox search screen instead of just returning all the files in a matter.

Major metadata removal programs such as Metadata Assistant (Payne Consulting) and iScrub (Esquire Innovations) integrate with Outlook and Worldox.

There are two programs designed specifically to work with Worldox that deserve mention:

- A relatively new program from Australia, **inMailX** adds significant functionality to the Outlook/Worldox integration. In particular, it adds metadata removal capability (including from PDF files) and lets you assemble a series of attachments into a single PDF file, order them as you will, and create a table of bookmarks for the file. It lets you limit the number of "conversations" (exchanges) when you print an e-mail so that instead of printing the entire series, you can print only the last one or two. It also somewhat simplifies the Worldox Quick Profiles functionality for sending e-mails to Worldox.

- **Symphony OCR**, part of Symphony Suite from Trumpet Inc., works specifically with the Worldox document store to apply OCR to documents as they are scanned and, depending on your settings, to apply OCR to your backlog of documents. Since Symphony OCR operates on a yearly page count (using the excellent Abbyy scanning engine), you need to verify carefully exactly how much you want to scan.

A companion module, Symphony Profiler, lets firms separate the process of making a Worldox "reservation" from the scanning process. Thus assistants or paralegals who are familiar with the firm's clients can set up how a document should be cataloged in Worldox, and a file clerk or other staff member can do the actual scanning (presumably at a lower hourly cost).

Legal Anywhere

Worldox now also integrates with Legal Anywhere, a leading provider of extranets. While Legal Anywhere provides a number of sophisticated services, the main functionality that concerns Worldox users is the ability to easily copy documents from Worldox to specified client/matter directories in the extranet system, as well as to define which clients and users can access the documents. Legal Anywhere uses a directory structure, not a Worldox-type profile group. Granular rights can be assigned to specific users and even to specific files (e.g., read only, copy, edit). Legal Anywhere can scrub metadata from documents copied to the extranet and prevent them from being copied or printed, if desired.

At the present time (mid-2013), document copying is a one-way operation. However, the ability to copy a client-modified document from the extranet back to Worldox as a version of the original document is under development and may be available by the time you read this.

See the Worldox website under "Solutions Partners" (http://www. worldox.com/worldox_partner_solutions) for a complete up-to-date list of available add-ins and companion programs.

Dropbox

There are "hooks" available that enable Worldox to integrate with Dropbox. These let you upload or download files to the Dropbox website.

An alternative method is to create a **Send To** to send files to a Dropbox folder on your local PC and let Dropbox synchronize the files from there. The problem with this approach is that you lose the integrity of the

Worldox system since you have a duplicate copy of the file in Dropbox that is not linked with Worldox and over which Worldox has no control.

Google Docs

Solo practitioners or very small firms can keep their Worldox documents in sync with the same documents in Google Docs. Based on one client's experience, it works like this:

- First, load the Google Docs add-in for Word that keeps Word files in sync with Google Docs.
- Create a document in Word, which syncs with Google Docs. Save it and it is profiled in Worldox. The two are in sync.
- Open the document from Worldox in Word. It syncs with Google Docs and is saved to Worldox. The two are still in sync.
- From a different terminal, edit the document over the web using Google Docs. Now the two documents are different. But open the document in Word/Worldox and it syncs up from Google Docs. When you save the document to Worldox, everything is back in sync.

NOTE   *All* users must do this for the system to work.

Where this system would break down would be in a larger firm if a single user did not have the Google Docs add-in loaded. When that user opens the document and saves it in Worldox, the changes go only to Worldox. If in the meantime someone opens the document in Google Docs and changes it, there are two conflicting sets of changes, and it is unclear which one will "win" the next time the file is opened from Word with the Google Docs add-in and synchronized with Google Docs.

In short, while this system could theoretically work, I wouldn't recommend that anyone use it for everyday production.

Worldox/Web Mobile

Worldox/Web Mobile, available at additional cost, lets you access your Worldox document store using any browser-based application or an iPad. As with most browser-based applications, the interface is similar to but not identical to the original version, and the functionality is somewhat limited. There are two main advantages:

- It lets you access Worldox from an iPad or a Mac client. There is a free app for iPad access to Worldox.

- It can be configured for use as a client portal so that (usually major) clients can access a selected subset of their documents.

You cannot use Worldox/Web Mobile to integrate Worldox with a smartphone other than via the browser. Worldox does not have a version optimized for smartphones.

Worldox GX3 Cloud

Worldox GX3 Cloud was released in early 2013. It is a full-featured, cloud-based version of Worldox. As a Software as a Service (SaaS) offering, it is available on a subscription basis. Unlike Worldox/Web Mobile, Worldox Cloud has an interface that is virtually identical with the Worldox network version. Further, Worldox Cloud integrates with *all* the desktop programs that the networked version does. In fact, when I was testing Worldox Cloud, I often forgot which version I was using. This integration is so unique among cloud-based programs that Worldox has applied to patent it.

In addition, Worldox Cloud has licensed Nuance PDF so that even very large PDF files are opened in the cloud and do not have to be downloaded. For multi-megabyte files, this can be a very substantial time savings.

Obviously, performance depends on your Internet connection.

Worldox Enterprise

Worldox Enterprise combines the standard network version (Professional) with the Cloud version. It requires additional server software (which must be purchased from Worldox) linked to your network and also runs Worldox Cloud in a private cloud (i.e., inside your firewall).

Thus when users are in the office, they use the network version of Worldox. When they are at home or on the road, they connect via the Cloud. Since the interfaces are identical, there is no confusion or need for training.

One ideal situation for this configuration would be in a midsize firm with small satellite offices in the same geographic region. The satellites might be "meeting offices" or only staffed part-time by one or two people. The firm is not interested in maintaining a full infrastructure for those places. Therefore, the main office would run the network version of Worldox and the outlying offices would connect using Worldox Cloud.

Conclusion

Worldox is the dominant document management system for small and midsize law firms, with over five thousand installed sites. Using Worldox will enable your firm to greatly increase users' efficiency, saving you time and money by making all your electronic files (including e-mails and scans) quickly searchable and retrievable. Think of Worldox as Google for your documents.

This book helps you take the next step beyond a "plain vanilla" installation so you can configure and use Worldox to get the optimal benefit from the program's features. It documents the many ways in which Worldox can be customized at an individual level, thus enabling users to work as they are most comfortable.

For the future, this book will also serve as a reference source as you continue to refine the ways in which Worldox helps you work.

Index

SELECTED BOOKS FROM THE LAW PRACTICE DIVISION

LinkedIn in One Hour for Lawyers, Second Edition
By Dennis Kennedy and Allison C. Shields
Product Code: 5110773 • LPM Price: $39.95 • Regular Price: $49.95

Since the first edition of LinkedIn in One Hour for Lawyers was published, LinkedIn has added almost 100 million users, and more and more lawyers are using the platform on a regular basis. Now, this bestselling ABA book has been fully revised and updated to reflect significant changes to LinkedIn's layout and functionality made through 2013. LinkedIn in One Hour for Lawyers, Second Edition, will help lawyers make the most of their online professional networking. In just one hour, you will learn to:

- Set up a LinkedIn® account
- Create a robust, dynamic profile--and take advantage of new multimedia options
- Build your connections
- Get up to speed on new features such as Endorsements, Influencers, Contacts, and Channels
- Enhance your Company Page with new functionality
- Use search tools to enhance your network
- Monitor your network with ease
- Optimize your settings for privacy concerns
- Use LinkedIn® effectively in the hiring process
- Develop a LinkedIn strategy to grow your legal network

Blogging in One Hour for Lawyers
By Ernie Svenson
Product Code: 5110744 • LPM Price: $24.95 • Regular Price: $39.95

Until a few years ago, only the largest firms could afford to engage an audience of millions. Now, lawyers in any size firm can reach a global audience at little to no cost—all because of blogs. An effective blog can help you promote your practice, become more "findable" online, and take charge of how you are perceived by clients, journalists and anyone who uses the Internet. Blogging in One Hour for Lawyers will show you how to create, maintain, and improve a legal blog—and gain new business opportunities along the way. In just one hour, you will learn to:

- Set up a blog quickly and easily
- Write blog posts that will attract clients
- Choose from various hosting options like Blogger, TypePad, and WordPress
- Make your blog friendly to search engines, increasing your ranking
- Tweak the design of your blog by adding customized banners and colors
- Easily send notice of your blog posts to Facebook and Twitter
- Monitor your blog's traffic with Google Analytics and other tools
- Avoid ethics problems that may result from having a legal blog

The Electronic Evidence and Discovery Handbook: Forms, Checklists, and Guidelines
By Sharon D. Nelson, Bruce A. Olson, and John W. Simek
Product Code: 5110569 • LPM Price: $99.95 • Regular Price: $129.95

The use of electronic evidence has increased dramatically over the past few years, but many lawyers still struggle with the complexities of electronic discovery. This substantial book provides lawyers with the templates they need to frame their discovery requests and provides helpful advice on what they can subpoena. In addition to the ready-made forms, the authors also supply explanations to bring you up to speed on the electronic discovery field. The accompanying CD-ROM features over 70 forms, including, Motions for Protective Orders, Preservation and Spoliation Documents, Motions to Compel, Electronic Evidence Protocol Agreements, Requests for Production, Internet Services Agreements, and more. Also included is a full electronic evidence case digest with over 300 cases detailed!

Facebook® in One Hour for Lawyers
By Dennis Kennedy and Allison C. Shields
Product Code: 5110745 • LPM Price: $24.95 • Regular Price: $39.95

With a few simple steps, lawyers can use Facebook® to market their services, grow their practices, and expand their legal network—all by using the same methods they already use to communicate with friends and family. Facebook® in One Hour for Lawyers will show any attorney—from Facebook® novices to advanced users—how to use this powerful tool for both professional and personal purposes.

Android Apps in One Hour for Lawyers
By Daniel J. Siegel
Product Code: 5110754 • LPM Price: $19.95 • Regular Price: $34.95

Lawyers are already using Android devices to make phone calls, check e-mail, and send text messages. After the addition of several key apps, Android smartphones or tablets can also help run a law practice. From the more than 800,000 apps currently available, Android Apps in One Hour for Lawyers highlights the "best of the best" apps that will allow you to practice law from your mobile device. In just one hour, this book will describe how to buy, install, and update Android apps, and help you:

- Store documents and files in the cloud
- Use security apps to safeguard client data on your phone
- Be organized and productive with apps for to-do lists, calendar, and contacts
- Communicate effectively with calling, text, and e-mail apps
- Create, edit, and organize your documents
- Learn on the go with news, reading, and reference apps
- Download utilities to keep your device running smoothly
- Hit the road with apps for travel
- Have fun with games and social media apps

Virtual Law Practice:
How to Deliver Legal Services Online
By Stephanie L. Kimbro

Product Code: 5110707 • **LPM Price:** $47.95 • **Regular Price:** $79.95

The legal market has recently experienced a dramatic shift as lawyers seek out alternative methods of practicing law and providing more affordable legal services. Virtual law practice is revolutionizing the way the public receives legal services and how legal professionals work with clients. If you are interested in this form of practicing law, *Virtual Law Practice* will help you:

- Responsibly deliver legal services online to your clients
- Successfully set up and operate a virtual law office
- Establish a virtual law practice online through a secure, client-specific portal
- Manage and market your virtual law practice
- Understand state ethics and advisory opinions
- Find more flexibility and work/life balance in the legal profession

Social Media for Lawyers: The Next Frontier
By Carolyn Elefant and Nicole Black

Product Code: 5110710 • **LPM Price:** $47.95 • **Regular Price:** $79.95

The world of legal marketing has changed with the rise of social media sites such as Linkedin, Twitter, and Facebook. Law firms are seeking their companies attention with tweets, videos, blog posts, pictures, and online content. Social media is fast and delivers news at record pace. This book provides you with a practical, goal-centric approach to using social media in your law practice that will enable you to identify social media platforms and tools that fit your practice and implement them easily, efficiently, and ethically.

iPad Apps in One Hour for Lawyers
By Tom Mighell

Product Code: 5110739 • **LPM Price:** $19.95 • **Regular Price:** $34.95

At last count, there were more than 80,000 apps available for the iPad. Finding the best apps often can be an overwhelming, confusing, and frustrating process. iPad Apps in One Hour for Lawyers provides the "best of the best" apps that are essential for any law practice. In just one hour, you will learn about the apps most worthy of your time and attention. This book will describe how to buy, install, and update iPad apps, and help you:

- Find apps to get organized and improve your productivity
- Create, manage, and store documents on your iPad
- Choose the best apps for your law office, including litigation and billing apps
- Find the best news, reading, and reference apps
- Take your iPad on the road with apps for travelers
- Maximize your social networking power
- Have some fun with game and entertainment apps during your relaxation time

Twitter in One Hour for Lawyers
By Jared Correia

Product Code: 5110746 • **LPM Price:** $24.95 • **Regular Price:** $39.95

More lawyers than ever before are using Twitter to network with colleagues, attract clients, market their law firms, and even read the news. But to the uninitiated, Twitter's short messages, or tweets, can seem like they are written in a foreign language. Twitter in One Hour for Lawyers will demystify one of the most important social-media platforms of our time and teach you to tweet like an expert. In just one hour, you will learn to:

- Create a Twitter account and set up your profile
- Read tweets and understand Twitter jargon
- Write tweets—and send them at the appropriate time
- Gain an audience—follow and be followed
- Engage with other Twitters users
- Integrate Twitter into your firm's marketing plan
- Cross-post your tweets with other social media platforms like Facebook and LinkedIn
- Understand the relevant ethics, privacy, and security concerns
- Get the greatest possible return on your Twitter investment
- And much more!

The Lawyer's Essential Guide to Writing
By Marie Buckley

Product Code: 5110726 • **LPM Price:** $47.95 • **Regular Price:** $79.95

This is a readable, concrete guide to contemporary legal writing. Based on Marie Buckley's years of experience coaching lawyers, this book provides a systematic approach to all forms of written communication, from memoranda and briefs to e-mail and blogs. The book sets forth three principles for powerful writing and shows how to apply those principles to develop a clean and confident style.

iPad in One Hour for Lawyers, Second Edition
By Tom Mighell

Product Code: 5110747 • **LPM Price:** $24.95 • **Regular Price:** $39.95

Whether you are a new or a more advanced iPad user, *iPad in One Hour for Lawyers* takes a great deal of the mystery and confusion out of using your iPad. Ideal for lawyers who want to get up to speed swiftly, this book presents the essentials so you don't get bogged down in technical jargon and extraneous features and apps. In just six, short lessons, you'll learn how to:

- Quickly Navigate and Use the iPad User Interface
- Set Up Mail, Calendar, and Contacts
- Create and Use Folders to Multitask and Manage Apps
- Add Files to Your iPad, and Sync Them
- View and Manage Pleadings, Case Law, Contracts, and other Legal Documents
- Use Your iPad to Take Notes and Create Documents
- Use Legal-Specific Apps at Trial or in Doing Research

30-DAY RISK-FREE ORDER FORM

ABA**LAW**
PRACTICE
DIVISION
The Business of Practicing Law

Please print or type. To ship UPS, we must have your street address.
If you list a P.O. Box, we will ship by U.S. Mail.

Name

Member ID

Firm/Organization

Street Address

City/State/Zip

Area Code/Phone (In case we have a question about your order)

E-mail

Method of Payment:
☐ Check enclosed, payable to American Bar Association
☐ MasterCard   ☐ Visa   ☐ American Express

Card Number   Expiration Date

Signature Required

MAIL THIS FORM TO:
American Bar Association, Publication Orders
P.O. Box 10892, Chicago, IL 60610

ORDER BY PHONE:
24 hours a day, 7 days a week:
Call 1-800-285-2221 to place a credit card
order. We accept Visa, MasterCard, and
American Express.

EMAIL ORDERS: orders@americanbar.org
FAX ORDERS: 1-312-988-5568

VISIT OUR WEB SITE: www.ShopABA.org
Allow 7-10 days for regular UPS delivery. Need it
sooner? Ask about our overnight delivery options.
Call the ABA Service Center at 1-800-285-2221
for more information.

GUARANTEE:
If—for any reason—you are not satisfied with your
purchase, you may return it within 30 days of
receipt for a refund of the price of the book(s).
No questions asked.

Thank You For Your Order.

Join the ABA Law Practice Division today and receive a substantial discount on Division publications!

Product Code:	Description:	Quantity:	Price:	Total Price:
				$
				$
				$
				$
				$

**Shipping/Handling:		***Tax:**		
$0.00 to $9.99	add $0.00	IL residents add 9.25% DC residents add 6%	**Subtotal:**	$
$10.00 to $49.99	add $6.95		***Tax:**	$
$50.00 to $99.99	add $8.95		****Shipping/Handling:**	$
$100.00 to $199.99	add $10.95	Yes, I am an ABA member and would like to join the Law Practice Division today! (Add $50.00)		$
$200.00 to $499.99	add $13.95		**Total:**	$